THE HISTORY OF SALT

BY
EVAN MARLETT BODDY

LONDON
1881

CONTENTS

CHAPTER I.

INTRODUCTION.

How frequently it happens that those natural productions with which we are to a certain extent superficially familiar, are to a great many not only uninteresting, but are regarded as subjects more or less beneath their notice; and by others as deleterious to the human race, and therefore to be cautiously used or scrupulously avoided. Another peculiarity is, that the more we are accustomed to them, the more our interest wanes, and probably at last degenerates into apathetic indifference.

We can only attribute these ignorant conceits and apparently unaccountable obliquity of judgment to two causes: an assumption of wisdom, and an unenlightened mind, unwilling to learn and loath to improve. Another hindrance which to a considerable extent precludes the study of what one may truthfully designate every-day subjects, is the restless *furor* for artful counterfeits of science, which are nothing else than the emanations of vain and visionary minds mixing together, as it were, an amalgam of truth and error. The present age is wonderfully productive of these eccentric ideas, while at the same time it is unhappily pregnant with the most unnatural and anti-healthful habits. The mystified authors take good care to run into the wildest extremes, so that their marvellous schemes and quaint devices (fortunately for their fellow-creatures) cause them to be justly derided by the thoughtful and disregarded by the sensible, though not a few are caught by the tinsel.

The grotesque aberrations of thought which have so prolifically generated such an incongruous medley of medico-social phantasmagoria, though considered by their promoters as wonderful scientific projections, are rendered more ridiculous than they really are, by their wild and unreasonable denunciations of those who do not happen to coincide with their farcical puerilities and whimsical crudities; and their intolerant followers, with considerable more zeal than discretion, promulgate their doctrines with voluminous additions and preposterous assertions—*mentis gratissimus error*.

These parodies of science have exerted as yet no material influence on modern thought, though there is a visible impress observable here and there; and they doubtless will ultimately collapse, like alchemy and other illusions of a bygone age, and in due time will fall as ignominiously before the resistless onslaughts of true science and knowledge, as those deceptive will-o'-the-wisps were finally extinguished, after whisking about for some centuries, by the calm, dignified, and logical condemnation of philosophical and scientific investigation. Need I remind my reader that I am referring to spiritualism, homœopathy, vegetarianism, and various other bastard distortions of science, though their purblind believers may regard them as legitimate offspring, and therefore deserving of due respect and consideration. Such imaginative plerophory is invariably antagonistic to scientific conclusions and common-sense principles, beside being redundant of inane folly and trivial hyperbole.

One of the peculiar crazes of the day, though it is not so universal as those to which I have just referred, is the unhealthful and insensate antipathy to salt, which has infatuated, in a greater or lesser degree, the several strata of society: some going so far as to proscribe it altogether, whilst others use it as if it were destructive to life, or at least subversive of health, and others assert that it originates disease! Some time ago I saw a letter in a temperance journal (we know that the advocates of total abstinence are frequently guilty of degrading their good cause by descending to frivolity), advising total abstention from salt; the writer, with amusing self-complacency, accused it of producing evils of an astounding nature—such is the latitude of pragmatical ignorance and silly egotism. The palpable absurdity of such an argument must be apparent even to the most careless thinker; it is with the view of exposing such a fallacy, both injurious and irrational, that I have written this treatise, and have been prompted to do so more especially as I find such ridiculous notions find great favour with those from whom better things ought to be expected.

I have laboured under many difficulties, owing to the meagre accounts concerning the history of this most important article of diet; no doubt arising from the fact that it has not been studied with that attention which it manifestly deserves; consequently I have been obliged to allude to the pages of Holy Writ, not that I wish to base my arguments on religion, but simply because we find therein the primary mention of salt, both as a purifying agent and as a condiment to food.

Reverting to the Bible on subjects of scientific import frequently brings down upon the author ill-timed ridicule, especially from those who profess a belief in nothing except their own crude notions; a fact which is surprising, for here we possess a Book which has stood the test of ages, which has weathered many a storm, which has victoriously emerged from many a conflict, and which has indeed passed through an ordeal which no other volume has been called upon to do—all indicative that it emanated from a mind immeasurably superior to that of man; and thus I am quite content to bear with any amount of satire, however pointed and keen, if I have it on my side of the question, which undoubtedly is the case respecting the medicinal and dietetic properties of salt: besides, when it is pronounced to be "good" by the Divine Speaker, one need not care an iota for those who assert that it is pernicious, however plausible or apparently logically conclusive their arguments may be.

CHAPTER II

HISTORY OF SALT.

I am approaching a subject somewhat novel and indeed difficult, and very probably it may be regarded by some as one far from being profitable or interesting; therefore I shall endeavour, though with some degree of diffidence, to consider it not only from a medical point of view, but to glance at some facts, both historical, geographical, and geological. By so doing, we shall be touching upon other matters not only pleasing but instructive, and which to a great many are but indifferently known; for though salt is to be almost universally seen on the tables of rich and poor alike, yet10 few are aware of its undeniable medicinal virtues, and many are totally ignorant of the great sustenance they derive from this indispensable and undoubtedly savoury condiment, besides being but moderately acquainted with its history. At the present time it is used nearly all over the world, and is acknowledged to be at least an adjunct necessary for perfect cookery; it is in requisition in fact everywhere, and even those who do not use it would be considered as lacking in taste were they to discard it altogether from their tables.

All, however, are to a certain extent cognisant of the fact of how insipid the daintiest dishes taste, if salt is omitted in their preparation, and the cook, however expert he may be in the culinary art, invariably fails in giving satisfaction (except to those whose palates are deranged or vitiated) if they are not seasoned with it; few, I think, will deny that animal food in particular is deprived of its pleasing flavour if it be eaten without salt. Those who have an unnatural aversion to it should bear in mind that the ingestion of improper animal and vegetable food frequently occasions many severe attacks of illness, and invariably provokes and intensifies that universal complaint, dyspepsia. George Herbert tells us in his *Jacula Prudentum*, that "Whatever the father of disease, ill diet is the mother;" and if food is taken into the stomach without its proper portion of salt, it is not what one would consider as wholesome; on the contrary, it is most decidedly "ill diet:" and being such, the system does not derive that kind of nutriment suitable for the promotion of a healthy action of the organs of the body, neither are the secretions in such a condition as is compatible with health. Physiologists inform us that the saliva holds salt in solution, and that it is also present in the gastric juice, which indicates at once how highly necessary it is for the system to be regularly supplied with it; for it is a physiological fact that the process of deglutition and digestion is partly due to the disintegrating and solvent action of these two secretions on the food, especially the latter; and consequently if the nutritious particles are to be absorbed in a state fit to make up for the waste of tissue, they ought to contain a sufficient amount of the chloride of sodium to take the place of that which has passed off through the media of the skin and the kidneys.

With these self-evident facts and a few physiological data before them (which really require no great effort to prove, so plain are they in their simple truth), all indeed must, or should be, convinced of the necessity of a liberal and judicious use of a substance which plays such an important part in the animal economy, and into which we shall enter more fully when we come to consider the relation which salt bears to food while it is going through the process of digestion.

Owing to the peculiar and incomprehensible prejudices of those who labour under the false impression that they are wiser and more discriminating than others, and who become proportionately obstinate in their notions, we shall endeavour to bring forward undeniable evidence in support of our arguments, though it is possible they may neither acknowledge that they are wrong, nor admit that their preconceived ideas prevent them from arriving at an unbiased conclusion. To such I have no hesitation in saying that they are much deceived if they imagine that the habit of abstaining from salt is contributive to health; such crabbed and confined views, however, are significant of the fact that human nature is frequently antagonistic to, and at cross purposes with, that which is ordained by the laws of nature to be beneficial.

I shall pass over the merits of salt as a seasoning to food, as it is my object to consider it solely in its relation to the animal economy, its operation in certain morbid conditions of the system, and its great importance as a health-preserver. But before proceeding, it will be as well to give a passing glance at its history and other attractive matter with which it is indirectly in relation; for though our investigations will be rather of a tentative character, and in a degree speculative, they may at least be interesting if not instructive. Perhaps others may be stimulated to penetrate deeper into the almost impenetrable obscurity with which the discovery of salt as a condiment is surrounded; and if they can bring to light who it was that primarily found out the chloride of sodium and utilised it as an adjunct to food, they will have solved a geological problem, and a long-standing historical enigma will be elucidated.

We possess no distinct and reliable data, and in fact no information of any kind, concerning salt in the early ages of the world as an article of diet, outside the pages of Scripture: all we really know, is, that in the infantile period of Europe, when the Indo-Germanic tribes entered it from Asia, though they were unacquainted12 with the sea, they were familiar with salt, as is proved by the recurrence of its name; yet whether they used it with their food we are by no means so sure of. The Kitchen-Middeners, who had their miserable dwellings on the wild shores of Jutland and similar inhospitable localities, *might* have been acquainted with it; but when we call to mind the nature of the food on which they lived, we may, I think, fairly conclude that they were ignorant of the use to which salt is now put; here again, however, we have only vague conjecture to fall back upon. The founder of Buddhism, Arddha Chiddi, a native of Capila near Nepaul, who subsequently changed his name to Gotama, and afterwards to Chakia Mouni, in his "Verbal Instructions," when dealing with his inquiry into the nature of man, asks us to consider what becomes of a grain of salt when cast into the ocean. Of the epoch of Gotama, or Chakia Mouni, there is great diversity of opinion; the Chinese, Mongols, and Japanese fix it at B.C. 1000; the Cashmerians at B.C. 1332; and the Avars, Siamese, and Cingalese fix it at B.C. 600.

The reference which Gotama thus makes to salt shows us that he was familiarly acquainted with it, otherwise he would not have figuratively mentioned it.

We are completely in the dark regarding salt as a condiment till Moses, in the Book of Job, asks the pertinent question, "Can anything which is unsavoury be eaten without salt?" As this book was penned B.C. 1520, we may conclude with a tolerable degree of certainty that it was so used in the time of the great Jewish Law-giver, and as he was brought up in the court of Pharaoh, and was skilled in all the wisdom of the Egyptians, it would point to the probability that salt was in common use in that ancient country.

The *first* mention we possess of salt is when Moses refers to the Vale of Siddim, which is the Salt Sea. This vast reservoir was known as the Dead Sea, and is so to this day: so the Jews, who were commanded to use salt in their sacrifices, had a large 13natural depôt which afforded them a limitless supply of the necessary material for carrying on their worship, and likewise for individual consumption: they also mixed a certain amount of salt with their incense. The second reference is in relation to one of those extraordinary incidents with which the first five books of the Old Testament teem, and that is during the destruction of the "Cities of the Plain," when Lot's wife was turned into a pillar of salt for disobedience.

We also read of salt in the Iliad of Homer, and as he did not flourish till about B.C. 850, we must give the honour of marking it indelibly on the pages of history to Moses the Jew, who lived, if the above date is correct, 670 years anterior to the illustrious Father of epic poetry, and, if the Cashmerians are correct in their calculation, 188 years before Gotama gave to the world his eight hundred volumes, pointing out the path towards individual extinction or "Nirwana."

We may likewise conclude that as it was known to the sagacious Hebrew, the æsthetic Greek, and the imaginative Asiatic, it was no doubt equally well known to the Egyptians, and probably amongst the neighbouring African tribes, long before the arrival of Joseph in the land of the Pharaohs, and centuries before the Oracle of Delphi was instituted.

From the following lines we may justly conclude that the Greeks looked upon salt as sacred, and used it as a thank-offering, and that it even was an absolute necessity to go through the ceremony of washing their hands before touching it; such extreme care and scrupulous observance indicates that it was a substance held in the highest reverence:

"At this the Sire embraced the maid again,

So sadly lost, so lately sought in vain.

Then near the altar of the darting King,

Dispos'd in rank their hecatomb they bring;585

14With water purify their hands, and take

The sacred off'ring of the salted cake;

While thus with arms devoutly rais'd in air,

And solemn voice, the Priest directs his pray'r."

Pope's *Homer's Iliad*, book i.

"And Menalaus came unbid, the last.485

The chiefs surround the destined beast, and take

The sacred off'ring of the salted cake:

When thus the King prefers his solemn pray'r."

Ibid., book ii.

"Achilles at the genial feast presides,

The parts transfixes, and with skill divides.

Meanwhile Patroclus sweats the fire to raise;

The tent is bright'ned with the rising blaze:

Then, when the languid flames at length subside,

He strows a bed of glowing embers wide,280

Above the coals the smoking fragments turns,

And sprinkles sacred salt from lifted urns."

Ibid., book ix.

At the time of the Exodus, Egypt was the great disseminator of knowledge, the centre of civilisation, and the emporium of trade, being then at its zenith of prosperity and power; and the countries which were conterminous no doubt regarded it with feelings of admiration and emulation, and were only too desirous to adopt its customs, as well as to avail themselves of the learning and culture which were only to be found in the land of obelisks and pyramids. Even the Greek philosophers were fain to acknowledge that Egypt was their storehouse of wisdom and æsthetic art; neither Athenian, Spartan, or Corinthian, ever disavowed his presumed Egyptian descent: and if history is to be relied on, the first King of Attica was a citizen of Sais; though this is a disputed point, for not only is the country of Cecrops a topic for controversy, but even his very existence is questioned, and by some altogether denied. This legend, if it is such, however, tends to show that the communication between the two countries (though of the two, Egypt was much more exclusive) was frequent; however, it is still a theme upon which classical commentators continue to exercise their controversial dexterity, some of whom affirm that there is no foundation for the myth. Yet many philosophical authors who flourished in Athens believed implicitly in the Egyptian genealogy of Cecrops; so that there is no 15reason why it should be stamped as fictitious, especially when it is verified by those who lived closer to that period of time than the incredulous moderns, whose great delight is to hint that many past historical events are incredible, and therefore apocryphal. I think we may certainly conclude that the sage discriminating Athenians were acquainted with their Egyptian descent, for they were the last people to believe in uncertainties, save such as were connected with their religion; and what nation is there, I should like to know, which is not similarly imposed upon by its own strange credulity, and the artful designs of schemers in this particular?

Cecrops, no doubt, while he introduced Egyptian arts and sciences into his adopted country, was too wise, and too well conversant with such an important commodity as salt, to forget both its existence and utility, on his arrival in the peninsula. Presuming for one moment that the emigration of Cecrops from Egypt is a fable, it is indicative of the fact that a perpetual intercourse, though of a modified nature, existed between that country and Greece. We know, however, that both Egyptian and Grecian histories, about the period of Cecrops, are involved in much obscurity and uncertainty (particularly as regards dates); and if, therefore, Cecrops and his foundation of a Pelasgic colony in Attica is a mythological tale, we may justly infer that Greece, owing to the greater antiquity of Egypt, imitated many of the social customs which were in vogue in the ancient and luxurious cities of the Nile.

We are also aware that at this early age, with a few brilliant exceptions like Egypt (we possess no reliable records of China, Japan, or Hindostan) the world was in a state of mental stagnation—chaotic is more descriptive: the thoughtful and mystical Egyptians were really the only recipients and parsimonious (if historical accounts are to be credited) disseminators of knowledge to their neighbours.

Many centuries later, we find a very remarkable instance of this influence of Egypt, which, though of a religious character, bears indirectly on our subject, by exemplifying this intellectual supremacy; the worship of Isis was established even in Imperial Rome herself, and we are told that the goddess was a most popular divinity amongst the wealthy citizens, a temple being erected to her honour in the Campus Martius; while she was designated by her enthusiastic worshippers, Isis Campensus. Now, though an Egyptian goddess was admitted with so much apparent readiness to occupy such an exalted position in the capital of the empire, when the Romans, with supercilious toleration, allowed the worship of as many gods as the people chose to venerate, yet the fact of building a temple for her exclusive worship, when all the other gods and goddesses were mixed and scattered hither and thither, without the slightest regard to order or attributes, is sufficient proof to substantiate the truth of my argument; and again if we call to mind the jealous pride of the Romans, and their disinclination to conform to the habits and customs of the countries which succumbed to their iron will, the admission of Isis to such elevated and almost unprecedented honours, would tend to show that many customs of Egyptian origin were not only adopted by the haughty Roman, but also by the Jew, Greek, Assyrian, and Persian, with a willingness in proportion to their utility, ornamentation, and agreeableness; and in some instances in deference to the intellectual ascendancy and scientific acquirements of this ancient people.

The Egyptians, owing to the central position of their country, the knowledge they were known to possess, their unrivalled skill in irrigation, the sublimity of their architecture, the abstruse wisdom of their priests, the mysterious erudition of their astrologers, and their wonderful agricultural proficiency and renown, caused their country to be frequently visited (sometimes by stealth, owing to their stringent laws against the admission of foreigners) by Greeks, Phœnicians, Assyrians, and Chaldeans, and indeed by all who professed the study of science, learning, and philosophy; so that we may be sure they very naturally carried back to their respective countries many of the domestic customs, as well as the knowledge 17of their learned entertainers and instructors. The great city of Thebes stood to Ethiopia, as well as to Egypt, in the same relation as that occupied by Rome to mediæval Christendom: the construction of her temples and palaces, and the vast population of priests and their thousands of attendants, in addition to the presence of the court, must have attracted thither multitudes of merchants, artists, artisans, and indeed travellers from all parts; for it was the centre in those days of civilisation and commerce; and it was easy of access, for an opening in the Arabian Sea afforded communication with the port of Kosseir on the Red Sea; while on the other side, the city was the best starting-point for the caravan routes across the desert to the three chief *oases* (the Greater, the Lesser, and that of Ammon), and to the interior of Africa. Thus Egypt, through Thebes, commanded the trade with India, and with the gold, ivory, and aromatic districts; and the mines of the neighbouring limestone hills added to her enormous wealth, and gave employment to thousands.

There is another point which we must not overlook, and that is, the Egyptians did not remain secluded in their own country, though they were jealous of the entry of strangers. They were a courageous and seafaring people (though much inferior in that respect to the adventurous Phœnicians), as far as the times went; for they engaged in many nautical enterprises after Psammetichus, about B.C. 670, had completely overthrown the ancient system of isolation, showing their dormant marine proclivities, which had hitherto been but secretly indulged in. Before these barriers had been broken down, their expeditions, as far as we know, never extended beyond the ancient Pillars of Hercules, which was regarded as an extraordinary exploit in those days (so we are told). One thing we may be practically certain of—wherever they went they carried with them not only their learning, but also their own peculiar customs and habits; and doubtless they experienced a satisfaction and pride in displaying their superiority not only in matters appertaining to knowledge, but also in civilisation. May we not justly infer that in their peregrinations they promulgated the utility and advantages of such a valuable commodity as salt wherever they went, wherever they settled? And would not the various peoples whom they visited, after having once experienced the palatableness of salt, take to it with an eagerness approaching avidity? The follow18ing paragraph, which I have extracted *in extenso* from the work of a highly gifted American author, and which is, I am proud to say, confirmatory of my own observations, delineates in a most forcible and graphic style the wonderful pitch of excellence in the sciences to which the Egyptians had attained, and their remarkable approach to the goal of indefectibility.

"The hieroglyphic writing had passed through all its stages of formation; its principles had become ascertained and settled long before we gain the first glimpse of it; the decimal and duodecimal systems of arithmetic were in use; the arts necessary in hydraulic engineering, massive architecture, and the ascertainment of the boundaries of land, had reached no insignificant degree of perfection. Indeed, there would be but very little exaggeration in affirming that we are practically as near the early Egyptian as was Herodotus himself. Well might the Egyptian priests say to the earliest Greek philosophers: 'You Greeks are mere children, talkative and vain; you know nothing at all of the past.'"

There is another channel which we will now take into consideration: the Philistines, who are supposed to have been descended from the Hycksos, or Shepherd Kings of Egypt, must have carried with them not a few of those customs which were in fashion amongst the sons of the founders of the gloomy temples of Memphis and Luxor; and on their expulsion by the regenerated Egyptians they were probably much assimilated with them, owing to many years' intercourse, and being located in the same country, though their nationalities were entirely distinct and their habits antagonistic, and notwithstanding the dislike the Egyptians had for, and their abhorrence of all those who were connected with, the grazing and the breeding of cattle; for whenever two nations mix promiscuously, however limited it may be, they are sure to adopt more or less each other's peculiarities, both in language and customs. These Philistines, when they emigrated on their defeat, took with them Egyptian civilisation, and the various tribes surrounding their newly acquired territory were very soon initiated into customs of which, perhaps, they were previously ignorant. There is nothing to prove this, but we may certainly surmise as much, if only by inference.13

19

Though we possess no historical record, we may, owing to the influence which Egypt doubtless exerted over the civilised parts of Europe, come to the conclusion that through her instrumentality the use of salt was made known to the surrounding nations and tribes; the sons of Jacob and their families were not sufficiently numerous to render them important in the estimation of their neighbours, nor were they powerful enough to extort respect or generate emulation.

We learn from Herodotus, who was born B.C. 484, that the Egyptians eat salted food, but nothing as regards using it in the same way as we do. He says, "They live on fish, raw, but sundried, or steeped in brine; they eat also raw quails and ducks, and the smaller birds, salted beforehand."14 The climate of Egypt, being remarkably dry and hot, would soon cause the decomposition of fresh animal food, and the Egyptians doubtless were aware of the fact that a prolonged immersion in brine or salt would be a complete deterrent; therefore there is no reason to doubt but that it was as common a custom amongst them as it is amongst us at the present day.15 The "Father of History" does not mention that salt was used as a condiment; though we may presume as much.

We might feel inclined at first to ascribe the honour of promulgating the utility of salt to the Hebrews, owing to the fact of one of their nation being the first to mention it, and of our possessing no other record of so early a date. Abraham was very probably cognisant of the virtues of salt, but though he was the founder of the people whose mission and chief delight was indiscriminate massacre, he was not one of them, but a Chaldean, a people famed for their wisdom; besides, he was the progenitor of two nations, viz. the Hebrews and the Ishmaelites, so that if Isaac was acquainted with the properties of salt, his half-brother Ishmael was equally so. Ishmael's descendants speedily developed into a free, independent nation, while Isaac's became slaves, and were made to construct costly monuments, build gigantic palaces, and raise majestic temples for their highly-cultured and imperious oppressors.

Which branch was likely to be imitated? Not the labouring, 20ignorant Hebrew, smarting under the lash of servitude, but rather the wandering Ishmaelite, who roamed at pleasure over the burning solitudes of Arabia; still, we must remember they were like a drop in the bucket when compared with their exclusive neighbours over the Red Sea. We are all aware that to this day the Eastern custom of placing salt before a guest is a token of amity and goodwill, and is significant enough to tell the visitor that he is for the time being in perfect safety; no Arab, even under provocation, would injure his most violent enemy after having once eaten salt with him under cover of his tent, till he was out in the desert.16 This custom has descended from generation to generation, and perhaps was instituted by the exiled son of Abraham and Hagar. This fact would seem to corroborate my hypothesis, that if the Jews, through Abraham, were aware of the properties of salt, their wild brothers of the desert were also acquainted with it, and from the same source. Where Abraham obtained the knowledge of salt rests in obscurity; he may have acquired the secret from the Egyptians, or, as he is termed the friend of the Founder of the Universe, probably he learnt it from a higher authority. I think we may dismiss the idea that we owe the discovery of salt to the Hebrews.

Our speculations on this point are, however, comparatively vain, for we cannot possibly determine who first discovered it, or who first utilised it as a condiment to food: all we really know is that it has become universal, and that from time immemorial; but whether the Egyptians, Chinese, or Hindoos first made use of it, will be one of those dark secrets the solution of which may interest the curious and ingenious, and test the patience and erudition of the profound. Such an investigation might probably be considered by some as unprofitable, even if it were attended with success. To such I do not think it will be unjust or irrelevant to observe that many scientific discussions which from time to time have occupied the learned world have been, as far as the results are concerned, not of much moment to humanity at large. For instance, of what practical utility is the modern theory of evolution, upon which so much erudition of a minute kind, and thought, is expended, except as indicative of the ingenuity of the author? Is science at all advanced when we are gravely told that the human organism springs 21from protoplasm, and that plastidules consist of carbon, hydrogen, oxygen, and nitrogen, and that they possess souls? It is true that these abstruse inquiries have been productive of inciting a greater desire for studying the workings of nature, and a great deal of which previous generations were profoundly ignorant has been ingeniously disclosed, and accurately elucidated, for one is bound to admit that, though in many instances their researches have failed in their ultimate results, they have been the indirect cause of giving a remarkable impetus to scientific investigation. Many recondite subjects have thus been exhaustively analysed, unintentionally, owing to the anxiety and eagerness of the authors to arrive at the goal of their wishes; for while they are seeking for that which probably will never be found, they discover others which, to all intents and purposes, very likely would never have been conceived of. Perhaps these remarks may be considered unjust and hypercritical as regards their researches into the mysteries of life, and do not appear to give sufficient importance to those philosophical deductions and enunciations, which the authors no doubt demand as an imperative right; for scientific physicists are apt to be tyrannical, and are not over-endued with the virtue of practicality, and naturally do not like their opinions and metaphysical reveries relegated to that region which Milton humorously baptized the "Paradise of Fools," but prefer their speculations to be regarded as irrefragable facts. As this is, however, the age for far-fetched theories, I think we may be allowed with perfect fairness to discuss a subject which has partially escaped the eyes of the inquisitive; and if it is not treated so elegantly as the learned theses of the leaders of science and philosophy of to-day, I cannot help thinking that we may probably gain considerably more by studying a subject which is practically of interest to all, than attempting to penetrate into the invisible and undefinable mechanism of biology.

Notwithstanding the proofs (vague though they be), which I have already mentioned to show that we are indebted to the Egyptians for the discovery of this most valuable substance, I nevertheless do so with diffidence, because they are of a hypothetical tendency, and consequently refutable.17 We may endeavour to trace the custom of using salt as a condiment to several nations, or even to one par22ticular nation, with as much earnestness as the modern speculatists attempt to account for unaccountable phenomena appertaining to the material and spiritual worlds; but, as far as the real evidence goes, we are as unsuccessful, and our inquiries almost as unsatisfactory, as theirs have been hitherto.

There is great probability, however, that the Egyptians first made known to other nations, directly and indirectly, the utility of salt, and that through their sole agency it was introduced into Europe through the media of commerce and other channels of communication, and no doubt, as I have previously stated, in deference to their superior wisdom. We learn from those scholars who are giving their attention to Egyptian remains, that Greece was indebted to Egypt for all her science, architecture, literature, art, and mythology; and, indeed, her domestic life was derived from that venerable country. "From Egypt, it now appears, were derived the prototypes of the Greek architectural orders, and even their monuments and conventional designs; thence came the models of the Greek and Etruscan vases; thence came many of the ante-Homeric legends ... thence came the first ritual for the dead, litanies to the sun, and painted, or illuminated, missals; thence came the dogma of a queen of heaven!"[18]

In confirmation of this we are told that Moses, as I have before remarked, was skilled in Egyptian wisdom: this is most emphatic, and we cannot but conclude that that wisdom was in a high state of perfection; and their works, which are still the surprise and admiration of travellers, testify to the truth of Holy Writ. Do not their monuments, which have set time at defiance, prove that they were a people highly gifted? Their ruins are more sublime than any other architectural remains which are extant, excelling, both in magnificence and magnitude, the classic temples of Greece, and the elegant buildings which once graced the banks of the golden Tiber. In reference to this I may quote Dr. Lepsius, who states that "all the principal cities of Egypt were adorned with temples and palaces.... These temples were filled with the statues of gods and kings, generally colossal, and hewn from costly stones."

Possibly, owing to the fact that salt is valued almost universally, and is a substance which has been demonstrated by experience to be necessary to humanity, it may have been, for all we can say, as well known to the Antediluvians as it is to us; and if so, then we are indebted to Noah. But these are but surmises; we really possess 23no authentic record, except that which we find in Holy Writ: and, with my reader's leave, we will now proceed to examine those passages of Scripture in which salt is mentioned.

We find that whenever salt is named, it is done so in language of a character stamping it as a most important essential; and especially do we notice this in the directions for the religious services of the Israelites. They were commanded in the most explicit language that in all their offerings they should "offer salt."[19] There is also another point which we must not omit, and that is, whenever salt is referred to in the Inspired Volume, it is invariably in connection with some important transaction: for example, when Elisha sweetened the waters of the fountain of Jericho, he cast salt into them; this act of the prophet illustrates, figuratively, the purifying properties of salt, for he said, "I have healed these waters."[20] When Abimelech captured Shechem, he strewed salt over the ruins;[21] and when Abijah harangued Jeroboam from the Mount Zemaraim, he speaks of a "covenant of salt."[22] We read farther on of this "covenant of salt" in the Book of Numbers.[23] In fact, in the Old Testament, as well as in the New, considerable stress is laid on this evidently important substance, which shows that nothing was considered as thoroughly accomplished if salt, in some way or other, was not intimately connected with it.

It was also a custom amongst the Hebrews, which was never departed from, to rub new-born infants with salt:24 this practice was in every respect healthy and cleanly, and if we Christians were wise we should, from a hygienic point of view, strictly follow a custom which is so conducive to health; for salt hardens the skin of newly-born children and renders it more firm, and prevents (unless there is an hereditary taint) any irritation or local eruption of the skin.

The first mention of salt as a condiment is to be found in Job;25 and as this beautiful book, which delineates the vicissitudes to which life is subjected, is supposed to have been written by Moses when he was dwelling amongst the Midianites, there is no doubt but that it was in general use not only in Egypt, but also amongst the surrounding nations. The answer to the question propounded by the persecuted man of Uz is the same now as it was three thousand years ago— there is nothing savoury without salt, and to a certainty there is no real permanent health without salt.

24

The Jews, like all Asiatic races, were much afflicted with various forms of leprosy, and as salt is an indirect antidote to cutaneous eruptions, they used it not so much as a condiment, but as a shield to ward off and protect them from those repulsive diseases which rendered those who were attacked obnoxious to their fellow-countrymen, by whom they were treated as outcasts till they had recovered from their loathsome maladies. To this day we find that by far the greater number who suffer from cutaneous diseases hardly ever eat salt with their food; this is an unquestionable fact, and truly significant of its inestimable virtue as an anti-morbific agent.

The Great Master says (and who will dispute such an unanswerable verity?) "salt is good;" and then He adds, "but if the salt has lost its saltness, wherewith will ye season it?"26 Addressing His disciples, He says: "Ye are the salt of the earth," and also, "Have salt in yourselves."27 These sayings prove in the most unmistakable language that salt is highly necessary. Our Saviour applies it in a religious sense, it is true, but He was too much of a philosopher, too great a logician, to use a metaphor of which the application could be shaken and disproved in the abstract, if the image or figure were fundamentally incorrect or inconsistent with the lesson which it was intended to convey; besides, He never would have declared it "good" had it been in the slightest degree provocative of anything deleterious to the human race, neither would He have made use of a figurative mode of speech if He could not have based it on a physical fact.

We are thus told in three simple words the value of salt, and none save the shallow, or the sophist, would attempt to prove the contrary. All must acknowledge the fact that salt is equally pleasant to the gourmand and the temperate; and that animal and vegetable food is not palatable without it. As it is pronounced to be "good" by the highest authority, we must regard it as one of Heaven's best gifts to man. It would be a comparatively small matter were it but a condiment rendering food more pleasant to the taste; but when we know that it is indirectly a preserver of health, and that it also contravenes the attacks of disease, its value will, I hope, be considerably increased.

I shall be more than satisfied if I am able to persuade those unwise people who make it a rule never to use salt, to resort to it at once without hesitation; for if they wish to be in a fair state of health, to have clear wholesome skins and fresh complexions, to be 25 free from intestinal parasites and cutaneous diseases, to have their digestive organs perform their functions compatible with health and personal comfort, they must have, practically speaking, salt in themselves.

We have thus, from very scanty records concerning salt, essayed to clear up, though very inconclusively, and I fear unsatisfactorily, certain points which have been unnoticed, by reason, I think, of the dense obtenebration with which the subject is surrounded; for it has hitherto baffled the researches of the geologist to discover its pristine source, and neither do we know who first used it as a condiment. The chemist can experimentalise with this inorganic substance to detect the presence of other bodies, and he knows its worth in the laboratory; but as for its origin, he is as much in the dark as the geologist.

CHAPTER III.

SALT AS A CHEMICAL, THERAPEUTICAL, AND TOXICOLOGICAL AGENT.

As a chemical agent, and from the manufacturing uses to which it is now put, salt is a most invaluable article from a scientific as well as from a commercial point of view. I will therefore draw the attention of my reader to its chemical properties; I will then allude to a few drugs which are partially derived from salt or the chloride of sodium; and will cursorily notice one great staple of commerce which owes the rapidity of manufacture to its sole agency, including some remarks on it as a poison.

Chlorine gas, which is obtained from the *chloride of sodium*, was discovered by Scheele in 1777, who named it *dephlogisticated muriatic acid*. Berthollet in 1785 termed it *oxygenated muriatic acid*. Sir Humphry Davy called it *chlorine* (from χλωρὸς, green) on account of its colour, and it has kept this name ever since. We thus see that salt is of great use to the chemist, for he not only obtains *chlorine* gas from it, but also *hydrochloric acid*, a most useful and efficacious drug in the treatment of some hepatic diseases. *Chlorine* also enters into combination with other chemical substances known as *chlorides* and *chlorates*, *sub-chlorides* and *per-chlorides*; for instance, we have the *chloride of ammonium* and the *chlorate of potash*; we also have the *sub-chloride of mercury*, or26 *calomel*, and the *perchloride of mercury*, or *corrosive sublimate*, with various others.

According to Pereira, *hydrochloric acid* was known to Djafar, or Geber, an Arabian chemist who flourished in the eighth century, and whom Roger Bacon calls *magister magistrorum*. Everyone is acquainted with the *chloride of lime*, a substance so generally used for household and disinfecting purposes, that I need only mention it; besides this, there are other salts with which *chlorine* enters into combination.

Formerly, to bleach cotton it was required to expose the material to the action of the sun and air, rendering the process long and tedious, as it took on the average quite six or eight months, and likewise a large surface of land was necessary for the operation.

Now, owing to *chlorine* gas, the process is completed in a few hours, and a comparatively small building is quite sufficient for the purpose; the fibre is beautifully and permanently whitened, and the manufacturer experiences the pleasing satisfaction of a more rapid remuneration.

Where would be our delicately white textile fibres were it not for the abundant and inexhaustible supply of salt? How should we be enabled to cause vegetable colours to vanish as if touched by the hand of a magician were it not for the bleaching properties of *chlorine*? And how should we be able to procure this green-coloured gas which produces these changes were it not for the *chloride of sodium*?

As a therapeutical agent *chlorine* possesses some characteristics peculiar to itself: it is used as a lotion for cancerous growths and foul ulcers, also for some cutaneous eruptions. It is likewise used as a vapour-bath; it has also been used in the treatment of chronic bronchitis and phthisis, and as a gargle in certain morbid conditions of the mouth. When *chlorine* is absorbed by the system it is supposed to possess some antiseptic and alterative action, acting specifically on the liver.

There is one more fact of a chemical nature in reference to chlorine which it would be unwise to throw aside, as it possesses some degree of interest. When the chemist wishes to decompose water, or in other words to liberate hydrogen from oxygen, he has no better agent to effect the purpose than this greenish-coloured gas, because it has such a strong affinity for *hydrogen*, which is one of the most characteristic properties of *chlorine*. Mix them together, and they combine with explosive violence if they are exposed to27 the beams of the sun. By this process we obtain *hydrochloric acid* gas, while the *oxygen* is liberated.

Chlorine only becomes active when it is associated with moisture; when dry it is quite inert as regards its bleaching powers, for "when moist it gradually decomposes the water, combining with its *hydrogen*, and disengaging its *oxygen*; and it is this *oxygen*, at the moment of its liberation, which is the really active agent in bleaching."28

Salt, like other inorganic compounds, has been known to act as a poison when taken in a large quantity, and Dr. Alfred Taylor, the eminent toxicologist, mentions a case in which a table-spoonful was taken by mistake for sugar; there was no vomiting or purging, but great pain in the region of the stomach, with dryness of the fauces, which lasted several days. Did not the above emanate from so great an authority, one would feel inclined to question it. Could anyone take such a large amount and swallow the same without being immediately aware of his mistake? Surely he would have immediately and spasmodically ejected it by reason of its extremely pungent character, before it had even reached the fauces.

Dr. Taylor says that "in a toxicological view it is not easy to distinguish the effects of common salt in these cases from the poisonous action of salt of sorrel, or binoxalate of potash, which it is well known may be taken with impunity in small quantity;" the symptoms are those of irritant poisoning, causing great pain and intensely inflaming the stomach and intestines, and in those few cases which we have on record the vomiting was excessive.

In France, though not hitherto, as far as I am aware, in Great Britain, several instances have occurred of severe sickness in particular localities, which have been traced to the adulteration of common salt with certain deleterious articles. In an investigation conducted by M. Guibourt some years ago, in consequence of some severe accidents which were presumed to have been produced apparently by salt in Paris and at Meaux, oxide of arsenic was detected; and this discovery was corroborated by MM. Latour and Lefrançois, who ascertained that the proportion of arsenic was sometimes a quarter of a grain per ounce. Another peculiar adulteration which was frequent was with the hydriodate of soda. At a meeting of the Parisian Academy of Medicine, held in December, 1829, an interesting report was read by MM. Boullay and Delens, subsequent to the inquiry by M. Sérullas, into the nature of a 28sample of salt which occasioned very extensive ravages. In the year 1829 various epidemic illnesses in several parishes were supposed to have originated from salt of bad quality, and in one month no less than 150 people in two parishes were attacked, some with nausea and pain in the stomach, slimy and bloody purging, some with tension of the abdomen, puffiness of the face, inflammation of the eyes, and œdema of the legs; and in some districts of the Marne one-sixth part of the inhabitants were affected in a similar manner. The salt being suspected, as it had an unusual odour somewhat like the effluvia of marsh land, it was analysed by M. Sérullas, and after him by MM. Boullay and Delens; the experiments of all three indicated the presence of one hundredth of its weight of hydriodate of soda, besides a small amount of free iodine. Owing to the discovery of arsenic by other experts in different samples of suspected salt, M. Sérullas repeated the analysis, but was unable to detect the slightest trace of that poison.

"M. Barruel states that he observed the occasional adulteration of salt with some hydriodate accidentally in 1824, while preparing experiments for Professor Orfila's lectures. He also found it in two samples from different grocers' shops in Paris. No satisfactory explanation has yet been given of the source of the adulteration with arsenic; but the presence of the hydriodate of soda has been traced to the fraudulent use of impure salt from kelp."[29]

It will be as well for us to know what pure salt really consists of, to the composition of which I now draw the reader's attention:

Composition of the Pure Chloride of Sodium.

	Atoms.	Eq. wt.	Per cent.	Ure.	Longchamps.
Sodium	1	23	39·3	39·98	39·767
Chlorine	1	35·5	60·7	60·02	60·233
	—	——	——	———	———
	2	58·5	100·0	100·00	100·000

MM. St. Claire Deville and Fouqué have shown that common salt can be resolved into its elements by the action of hot steam alone, which Lussa and other chemists had thought impossible.

Prof. Meyer, of Berne, has lately demonstrated by experiments on chlorine gas, that the assumption of its elementary character is an error, and that it is nothing more or less than the oxide of a metal which he calls *murium*. This discovery opens up an interesting question for physiological chemists to investigate; for if he is correct, chlorine is not an element, but is simply the oxide of a metal.

CHAPTER IV.

GEOGRAPHICAL DISTRIBUTION.

Salt, fortunately for us, is a commodity remarkably easy to obtain; almost everyone knows it is in great abundance in the ocean,[30] and there are inexhaustible supplies of it in the earth; it is also present in some rivers, and in no inconsiderable quantity. Mr. John Ashley, in the *Quarterly Journal of the Chemical Society,* in his "Analysis of Thames Water," tells us the exact amount:

Composition of Thames Water at London Bridge in grains per gallon of 70,000 grains.

Carbonate of Lime	8·1165
Chloride of Calcium	6·9741
Chloride of Magnesium	·0798
Chloride of Sodium (salt)	2·3723
Sulphate of Soda	3·1052
Sulphate of Potash	·2695
Silica	·1239
Insoluble Organic Matter	4·6592
Soluble Organic Matter	2·3380
	———
	28·0385

We may account for this great proportion of salts by the fact that the Thames collects its water from the drainage of comparatively soft and soluble rocks; we should also remember the vast amount of refuse organic and inorganic matter which is being continually thrown into this river; and we must also call to mind that it is nothing more or less than the main sewer which receives the ordure of the modern Babylon.[31]

We may naturally suppose that in those rivers which flow through sparsely inhabited countries, where there is little or no traffic, the amount of saline matter would be next to nothing, and probably not a trace would be discovered. In a river like the Thames, owing to the vast quantity of its shipping, the great percentage which Mr. John Ashley has given us need not afford the least surprise. Sea-water is deficient in its proper proportion of salt at the mouths of great rivers, where the volume of fresh water displaces that which properly belongs to the sea, and therefore a river does not obtain much saline matter from that source.

30

Before we pass on to consider the geographical distribution of salt, we will just cursorily glance at the position it occupies in the vegetable world. It is present in all plants growing near the sea, and in variable quantities in some of those which are in or near districts where the soil is mixed with salt; though its place is taken by potash when they grow inland. Dr. Balfour writes as follows: "Soda and potash occur abundantly in plants. They are taken up with the soil in combination with acids. Those growing near the sea have a large proportion of soda in their composition, whilst those growing inland contain potash. Various species of salsola, salicornia, halimœnenum, and kochia yield soda for commercial purposes and are called halophites (ἅλς, salt, and φυτὸν, plant). The young plants, according to Göbel, furnish more soda than the old ones. There are certain species, as Armeria maritima, Cochlearia officinalis, and Plantago maritima, which are found both on the seashore and high on the mountains removed from the sea. In the former situation they contain much soda and some iodine; while in the latter, according to Dr. Dickie, potash prevails and iodine disappears."

Soda being present in those plants growing near the sea, and potash in those which are inland, are two points well worthy of notice, and which we will now discuss. The number of vegetables which are cultivated near the coast shrink into insignificance when compared with those which grow inland; and naturally the markets are supplied with inland produce on account of a larger supply, therefore the consumption of those vegetables containing potash is in the same ratio. This being unquestionably the case, we ought, on that account alone, to use salt freely with our vegetable food in order to supply that which is absent, arising from the difference of locality and dissimilarity of the atmosphere. I shall enter fully into the relation salt bears to vegetable food while it is going through the process of digestion further on, when we come to consider the effects which food salted beforehand has upon the system when continued for any length of time, with little or no variation, which dietary is supposed to be the sole cause of the attacks of scurvy on board ship.

The sea is that grand reservoir which supplies the earth with its fertility; and the air and sun are mighty engines which work without intermission to raise the water from this inexhaustible cistern. The clouds, as aqueducts, convey the genial stores along the atmo31sphere, and distribute them in seasonable and regular proportions through all the regions of the globe.

With what difficulty do we extract a drop of perfectly sweet water from this vast pit of brine! Yet the sun draws off, every moment, millions of tons in vaporous exhalations, which, being securely lodged in the clouds, are sent abroad sweetened and refined, without the least brackish tincture or bituminous sediment; sent abroad upon the wings of the winds to distil in dews and rain, to ooze in fountains, to trickle along in rivulets, to roll from the sides of mountains, to flow in copious streams amid burning deserts and populous kingdoms, in order to refresh and fertilise, to beautify and enrich, every soil in every clime.

Though the ocean is salt, yet certain seas do not contain so much as others; my reader must not therefore conclude that the chloride of sodium, or salt, is equally diffused in sea-water, for the atmosphere receives a larger or lesser amount by reason of evaporation. Dr. Draper writes that the "temperature of the Mediterranean is twelve degrees higher than that of the Atlantic, and since much of the water is removed by evaporation, it is necessarily more saline than that ocean."

It is said that the southern seas are slightly more salt than the northern, the reason for which phenomenon has not been, as yet, satisfactorily explained.

It is strange that salt should determine the colour of the sea, and that for centuries the cause of this peculiar natural phenomenon of the ocean should have been a closed secret even to men of science. Even from the earliest times, the origin of this marine peculiarity has attracted the attention and wonder of navigators; yet, strange to say, it has only been discovered within the last few years. The many expeditions which have been despatched by the Governments of England, Germany, and others, for the express purpose of oceanic discovery, have been the means of solving a question which has perplexed all races of seamen from the time of the Phœnicians, and which astonished Columbus on his voyage to the Indies.

These recent scientific investigations have proved that the proportion of salt held in solution by sea-water determines its blue or green appearance, and also its specific gravity; consequently, when the water is blue, we may conclude that it holds a much greater proportion of salt; when it is green, it is indicative that there is a decrease.

32

There is one phenomenon which is peculiarly interesting. There are two kinds of ice floating in the Arctic and Antarctic seas—the flat ice and the mountain ice. The one is formed of sea-water, the other of fresh. The flat or driving ice is entirely composed of salt water, which, when dissolved, is found to be salt, and is readily distinguished from the mountain or fresh-water ice by its whiteness and want of transparency. This ice is much more terrible to mariners than that which rises in lumps. A ship generally can avoid the one, as it is seen at a distance; but it frequently gets in amongst the other, which, sometimes closing with resistless force, crushes the doomed vessel to pieces.

The surface of that which is congealed from the sea-water is not only flat, but quite even, hard, and opaque, resembling white sugar, and incapable of being slid upon.

Salt is found in variable quantities in different countries, and in various conditions; in one part it may be found as a huge mountain, in which there are dark and lofty caverns; in others it is deposited in marshes and lakes, and in others in deep mines, many hundreds of feet beneath the surface of the earth.

In some countries there are vast quantities of rock or fossil salt. Salt has been divided into *three* kinds: native or rock salt; common or sea salt, also called white-salt; and bay-salt. Under the title of bay-salt are ranked all kinds of common salt, extracted from the water, wherever it is dissolved by means of the sun's heat and the operation of the air. If sea-water is evaporated by means of a gentle heat we also obtain what is known as bay-salt. Common salt, or sea-salt, or white-salt, which is extracted from the sea, is composed of hydrochloric acid, saturated with soda, and is found in salt water and salt-springs, also in coal and gypsum-beds. "The sea itself, if desiccated, would afford a bed of salt five hundred feet thick, one hundred for every mile."

In England, and especially in Cheshire, there are large salt-mines, at Nantwich and Middlewich, which have existed ever since the Roman occupation of Britain; and in the year 1670 the Staffordshire salt-mines were discovered, and accordingly excavated. Those in Cheshire have been renowned for centuries; their great extent is such that the surface has subsided on account of its being undermined for so many miles.

"In England, the Trias is the chief repository of salt, or chloride of sodium; and brine-springs, which are subterranean streams of water impregnated with salt from percolating through saliferous33 strata, are abundant in the great plain of the red marls and sandstones of Cheshire. The salt, however, is not uniform in extent, but occupies limited areas." The saliferous strata of Northwich present the following series:

1. Uppermost calcareous marl 15 feet

2. Red and blue clays   120 "

3. Bed of rock-salt   75 "

4. Clay, with veins of rock-salt 31 "

5. Second bed of rock-salt   110 "

Droitwich, in Worcestershire, which is situated nearly in the centre of the county, has been celebrated for the production of salt from its brine-springs from the time of the Romans, who imposed a tax on the Britons, who, it appears, worked the mines; and also made salt a part of the pay of their soldiers' *salarium*, or salary. 32 Ever since, this inexhaustible fountain of saline water has continued flowing up, and yielding salt in undiminished quantities. It is very likely that the manufacture is coëval with the town itself; but it was not till the year 1725 that the strong brine for which it is now celebrated was discovered. From one spring, even, the enormous amount of one thousand tons of salt are obtained every week. At the depth of thirty or forty feet is a bed of hard gypsum, about one hundred and fifty feet in thickness; through this a small hole is bored to the stream of brine, which is about twenty-two inches in depth, and beneath this is the rock-salt. The brine rising quickly through the aperture is pumped into a capacious reservoir, whence it is conveyed into iron boilers for evaporation. It is supposed to be much stronger than any other in the kingdom, containing above one-fourth part its weight of salt. "One of the shafts is sunk to a depth of nearly five hundred feet, and passes through four layers of salt, eighty-five feet in aggregate thickness. Some of the beds of salt in Cheshire are from seventy to one hundred and twenty feet in thickness;" and it is sometimes so hard that it requires to be blasted with gunpowder.

In those districts where the marls of the Trias are covered by other beds, and the salt-springs force their way through the superincumbent deposits to the surface, these solutions of the chloride of sodium undergo a chemical change, acquiring other properties, and are then called mineral waters. The Cheltenham waters originate thus.33 Beneath the town of Cheltenham lie the Triassic deposits, 34the reservoir of the rock-salt and brine-springs, which generate the mineral waters, and from which they derive their saline ingredients. In their passage to the surface they go through various modifications, by reason of the superincumbent beds of Lias, which are impregnated with iron pyrites and the sulphate of lime. From the analyses of these waters, it appears that their principal constituents are the chloride of sodium (muriate of soda), or sea-salt, and the sulphates of soda and magnesia. Sulphate of lime, oxide of iron, and the chloride of magnesium are present in some wells only, and in much smaller quantities. Besides these ingredients, *iodine* and *bromine* have been detected by Dr. Daubeny, who instituted experiments to ascertain whether these two active principles, which the French chemists had recently discovered in modern marine productions, did not exist in mineral waters issuing from strata formed in the ancient seas. As the saline springs of the red marls rise up through the Lias they undergo certain chemical changes. From the decomposition of the sulphate of iron which takes place, a vast quantity of sulphuric acid must be generated, which, reacting on the different bases of magnesia, lime, etc., contained in the strata, forms those sulphates so prevalent in the higher or pyritous beds of the Lias; the oxide of iron being at the same time more or less completely separated. By this means the mineral waters, which are probably mere brine-springs at the greatest depths, acquire additional medicinal qualities as they ascend to the places whence they flow. At the same time, it must be borne in mind that fresh water is continually falling from the atmosphere upon the surface of the Lias clays, and percolating through the uppermost strata.34

The medicinal properties which are peculiar to these mineral waters will be considered further on, when we come to discuss the action of salt on the system, in health and disease, and the restorative results which are due solely to its instrumentality.

The salt district is in the line which joins the Severn, the Dee, and the Mersey, and doubtless once consisted of lakes flooded at every tide, which, drying at certain seasons and at low tides, deposited beds of salt, from Droitwich in Worcestershire, through Nantwich, to the Mersey; brine-springs flowing over beds of salt, or rock-salt, being found at different places on the entire line.

In the year 1863 a bed of rock-salt was discovered near the mouth of the Tees, at Middlesborough, and also on the Durham side of the river. The boring at Middlesborough showed that it 35was about 100 feet in thickness. Of late, borings have been made near Port Clarence, on the Durham side, but with what result I am not informed.

Scotland, as well as Ireland, is deficient in the more recent formation; for salt, as well as chalk, does not occur. Both are entirely absent; but geologists inform us that at one time chalk *did* exist, judging from the presence of flints in considerable quantities in Aberdeenshire, which they say affords unequivocal evidence of the former presence of cretaceous strata now integrated; and they account for it thus: the soft chalk being exposed to the action of the rain and storms, has been gradually washed away, while the flints which were embedded in it still remain. If this hypothesis is correct, that at one time chalk existed and is now absent, we may by inference, though we possess no evidence, presume that salt likewise, at some period or other, was present in this part of the United Kingdom. Chalk being entirely composed of the accumulation of marine shells ground to impalpable powder, which has been gradually consolidated, and being very rich in organic remains of shells, star-fish, sponges, fishes, and lizards, must have been deposited by sea-water, as its various ingredients indicate; therefore, during its deposition, salt, if originating from sea-water, must of necessity have left some marks characteristic of itself, in conjunction with the chalk; both being, more or less, intimately connected with sea-water, though the formation of one may not have been simultaneous with the formation of the other.35

In our lately acquired "gem of the sea," Cyprus, there have been found extensive lakes of salt near Larnaca, the capital, so that this liberally-abused island possesses at least something which may prove of pecuniary value to its present owners. Being for several centuries under the benighted rule of the Turk, this staple of commerce has been entirely neglected, so as not to have been of the slightest use to the inhabitants or to the greedy pachas.

In the south of Western Australia there are vast salt marshes which only require to be worked so as to become the means of enriching the colonists, and indirectly attracting emigrants to this hitherto unprofitable portion of a dependency of England. The principal, which is called Lake Austen, is 1400 feet above the level of the sea.

36

Salt is also to be found in our Indian Empire, in Rajpootana and elsewhere, and is of considerable value to that country, especially while it remains in the hands of the enterprising European; according to Mr. Wynne, there is a salt range which extends from Kalabagh to a point north of Tank. After acquainting us with its geographical position, he says: "The coincidence between the physical features and the geological structure of the ground is intimate, the axial lines of the mountains carrying on the Salt Range feature being also axes of anticlinals lying for the most part along the scarped acclivities presented towards the Indus plains. These plains are part of the great *quasi-desert* flat over which the Indus has in past times capriciously wandered towards the Arabian Sea. Whether they are due in any degree to marine explosion is uncertain, though the sea may very possibly once have covered the low ground in question. The ridges of the Salt Range, as they exist at present, doubtless mark the same great later, or post-tertiary, period of mountain-forming activity, in which originated not only the remainder of the Salt Range, but also the Western Himalaya and the Suliman and Afghan mountains." When we come to consider the geological bearings of salt, and its presumed origin, and other points in connection with it, I shall again revert to this highly interesting paper of Mr. Wynne's.

In the Deccan, half-way between Bombay and Nagpur, there is a very remarkable salt lake. It is a circular hollow, about one mile across, and from 300 to 400 feet deep, having at the bottom a shallow lake of salt water without any outlet. This hollow, I must tell my reader, is ascribed by scientific men to a volcanic explosion.

There are so many lakes of salt, which are completely isolated and so many miles from the sea, that it is next to impossible to account for their existence if we do not ascribe them to volcanic action. If they are situated in low-lying districts, we may justly presume that at one time the sea must have been present, or that the deposition must have resulted from occasional, or tidal, overflow of salt water; but when they are many miles from the coast, and many feet above or below the sea-level, then they may be due to volcanic agency; and we shall find further on several other salt lakes of variable depths or altitudes which would seem to corroborate this hypothesis. The sea is undoubtedly a most formidable agent in the disintegration of land, and often destroys whole tracts, forcing its resistless waves into the interior of continents, and then, owing to some unexplained cause, retiring to its original boundary.37 This may take centuries to complete, for revolutions effected by nature are not accomplished speedily, unless there is some sudden spasmodic upheaving, arising from earthquakes or storms. In 1282, the isthmus uniting Friesland with the north of Holland was totally destroyed by violent storms. In our own country a similar phenomenon occurred in the year 1475, when a large tongue of land at the mouth of the Humber was entirely broken up and carried away by the sea. In 1510 an irruption of the Baltic formed the Frische-Haff, an opening 6000 feet broad, and from twelve to fifteen fathoms in depth. The eastern coast of England is continually receding, owing to the encroachment of the sea. The rate of encroachment of the sea at Owthorne, in Yorkshire, is reckoned at four yards in every year, and several villages have been swallowed up by the ocean; and in like manner the cliffs of Norfolk and Suffolk are suffering a continual decay.

Though the sea is so destructive an element, it is also an agent in the reproduction of land. The rocks and sand washed away from one place are conveyed by tides and currents far into the sea, and are deposited in strata, and then, in course of time, form shoals and banks, which subsequently become promontories and islands. Alluvial land has thus been formed, and in a similar way have many of the stratified rocks been deposited; and as animals and plants have been carried away and imbedded in the deposits of rivers, or floods, so at some future period, though countless ages may elapse during the process, will such animals and plants be discovered deposited in these newer strata, just as we find organic remains in the older rocks. The gradual deposition of strata has been the work of an incalculable period of time, but the process may be traced every day in the sections of marine estuaries and lakes. Owing to this continual receding of the land in one part, and elevation of land in another, there is an incessant change, from which, though occupying many ages, and proceeding so slowly that it would be unobservable were it not for accurate investigation, we may easily conjecture that what is now land may at one time have been the bed of the ocean, and where the sea now sweeps with overpowering fury, there may once have been meadows and forests. The salt lakes, if not originating from volcanic force, no doubt are the remains of the great ocean, which, when it receded, left here and there, in what once were luxuriant valleys, large reservoirs, indicating that in bygone ages it had covered the land.

In Germany, Spain, Italy, Hungary, and Poland, there are exten38sive mines of rock-salt, and also in various other parts of Europe.36 There are also large mountains wholly composed of this fossil salt, two of which are in those provinces of Russia known as Astrakhan and Orenburg; and in the Crimea salt is said to be daily accumulating in the inland lakes. In Asiatic Russia there are extensive beds of salt, near Lake Indur, in lat. 48° 30′, long. 69°. The Caspian Sea, called by the Turks "Cozgoun Denghizi," "the sea of crows and cormorants," is "a great salt-water lake," according to Dr. William Smith, though Dr. Lemprière says that "its waters are sweet."

The most interesting salt-mine is that of Wieliczka, near Cracow, in Galicia; it has been celebrated for centuries, and has been worked for the last six hundred years. This wonderful mine is excavated in a ridge of hills at the northern extremity of the chain which joins the Carpathian mountains. When the stranger reaches the mine there bursts upon his view a little world, the beauty of which is scarcely to be imagined. He beholds a spacious plain containing a kind of subterranean city, with houses, carriages, and roads, all scooped out of one vast rock of salt, as bright and glittering as crystal, while the blaze of the lights continually burning for the general use is reflected from the dazzling columns which support the lofty arched vaults of the mine, which are beautifully tinged with all the colours of the rainbow, and sparkle with the lustre of precious stones, affording a more splendid and fairy-like aspect than anything above ground can possibly exhibit. In various parts of this spacious plain stand the huts of the miners and their families, some single, and others in clusters, like villages. They have very little communication with the world above them, and many hundreds of persons are born and pass the whole of their lives here.

Through the midst of this plain lies a road which is always filled with carriages laden with masses of salt from the furthest part of the mine. The drivers are generally singing, and the salt looks like a load of gems. A great number of horses are kept in the mine, and, when once let down, never see daylight again.

Such is the marvellous salt-mine of Wieliczka, which is more renowned on account of its magnitude, its age, and the weird and 39almost supernatural aspect it presents to the visitor, than any other. Those subterranean palaces, with their magnificent appurtenances, their fantastic occupants, and other dreams of the imaginative, are not more strange or astonishing to the fascinated reader of romance than this extraordinary, glistening, cavernous, mineral city, with its numerous lamps, its crystallised walls, its roads, and the plaintive songs of the drivers as they drive their horses through its sunless thoroughfares, presents to the eyes of the surprised traveller.

There are valuable mines of salt in France, and in Greece, near Missolonghi, but these have no special points of interest connected with them.

In Abyssinia there are extensive and inexhaustible beds of salt, which is used in quite a different way from what it is in other countries, for little bars of it are circulated in place of small coin; but it is only when it reaches the Amhara and Galla districts that it becomes valuable.37

In other parts of the African continent there are large mountains of rock-salt, and those of Tunis and Algiers are especially notable.

Salt is also to be found in Asia, in large mountains, in marshes, and in lakes, to some of which I have already alluded. In the north of Persia there is a large salt desert, and near Ispahan there are quantities of rock-salt. The island of Ormuz, in the Persian Gulf, almost consists of fossil salt; it is indeed so very plentiful that the atmosphere is completely charged with it, so that the dwellings of the inhabitants are encrusted with a tolerable thick layer, giving them a peculiar glistening appearance; this phenomenon is owing to the small particles of salt continually floating in the air and rising from the ground, much in the same way as we see dew deposited on the top of a garden wall or on a lawn after a hot summer's day.

We learn from Herodotus that there was a salt lake in Phrygia, in Asia Minor. "Having so said, and fulfilled his promise, Xerxes continued his route onwards. After passing by a city of Phrygia, called Anaua, and a lake out of which salt is produced, he came to Colossæ, a large city of Phrygia."38 I have previously alluded to the Dead Sea and the interesting phenomena which it presents; due south of it is the Valley of Salt.

40

There are salt springs and springs from inflammable gas in China, in long. 101° 29′, lat. 29°, near Thibet; and there is a large salt lake possessing the strange name of Tsomoriri, many feet above the level of the sea, in Western Thibet.39 "The Chinese bore well through the rocks, and prepare the salt by firing the gas of others, so that one heats 300 kettles by gas-fire." The celestials, with their habitual aptitude and industry, have obtained this salt for many centuries, and simply by this ingenious method.

As a fact illustrating the value of salt in Siberia, I may as well mention that in our own country a ton of salt is sold for fifteen shillings, whilst on the Yenesei river as much as fifteen pounds is given for the same quantity. The Muscovite we thus see is as acutely alive to the beneficent results of a free use of salt as a dietetic, as we English, and it would seem as if he were more so.

In some countries remote from the sea, which are devoid of salt-mines, and where the water is not impregnated with it, the inhabitants, aware of its usefulness, have a method of extracting it from the ashes of vegetables. This fact would certainly seem to indicate that salt has been used by various nations, as if mankind had an intuitive knowledge of the benefits arising from the use of salt, and that consequently, if there were no lakes containing it, or mountains from which they could procure it, they were determined to obtain it if even by artificial means.

As an illustration of the presence of salt in places distant from the sea, I need only refer to the Great Salt Lake of Utah, on the shores of which stand the Mormon city. Long before the founder of the Latter Day Saints thought of establishing a quasi-religious community, travellers who had the temerity to wander over the wild prairies of the Oregon, the home of the bison and the hunting-ground of the Indian, and who explored the secrets of the then unknown land of the "Far West," were struck with amazement at the glistening aspect of the surface; for in many places it was covered over with an impure kind of salt, apparently a combination of *muriate and sulphate of soda*,40 or more 41probably an impure form of the *chloride of sodium*. On tasting the water which had collected in numerous little pools of no more than a few inches in depth, they found it so bitter and pungent that it acted on the mucous membrane almost as powerfully as a corrosive poison. This large tract of country was at that time teeming with life, for they daily saw vast herds of bisons, and frequently came upon the hidden towns of the prairie-dog; in fact, wherever they went, they either crossed the path of these wild denizens of the plain, or else the sky was darkened by innumerable flocks of birds. The district was wonderfully healthy, and totally free from malaria or other causes generative of disease; the Indians, too, were splendid specimens of humanity; they had not as yet been tainted by too close a proximity with the so-called superior civilisation of the white man, neither had they been so unfortunate as to have fallen a prey to the vices and diseases which generally accompany the humanising European.

On the pampas of La Plata, which is the treeless abode of the wild horses of South America, there are several salt lakes, not many miles distant from the river Quinto, and over these boundless wastes thousands of wild cattle and horses gallop at pleasure, and afford an inexhaustible stock of game for the lasso of the fearless and expert Gaucho. Now it is a well-authenticated fact that those diseases which are so destructive to the horses and cattle of Europe are almost unknown in these regions. I do not mean to assert that these salt lakes of La Plata account for the exemption which this district enjoys from equine diseases; but there is no doubt that the exhalations from them purify the atmosphere, and that their influence extends for many miles because of the open nature of the country. As a natural result, the whole region is constantly kept in a healthy state; for air, charged with the chloride of sodium, must of necessity act as a preventive to everything inimical to health, and pure air we know (though how few really know what that blessing is) is of a paramount importance in the rearing of cattle. The foot-and-mouth disease, comparatively, has never played such havoc as it does in Europe, and pneumonia, which is almost intractable to treatment in this part of the world, and which is frequently fatal when it is complicated with inflammation 42of the pleura, hardly ever appears in these parts, where stables and farms are not far off from being rudimentary in construction, and would appear to an English farmer, accustomed to the cosy-looking farmsteads of his own country, very ill-calculated for successful farming, and not at all adapted for bringing his cattle and horses to perfection; yet it is just the reverse, for there is no other part of South America so well fitted for the breeding of cattle, and there is no other locality, whether in the Old or New Worlds, so completely free from disease as the open pampas of La Plata.

CHAPTER V.

GEOLOGICAL FORMATION OF SALT.

Sir Isaac Newton, in his incomparable work upon Optics, likens a particle of salt to a chaos, because of its "being dense, hard, dry, earthy in the centre; and rare, soft and moist in the circumference." This ingenious definition is what one would expect from such an observant and profound investigator; and I do not think that we shall be able to find a better description of a salt-crystal than that which this great philosopher has bequeathed us.

Regarding the original formation of rock-salt, there are many opinions, theories and conjectures, and to the present day it is an undecided question. We are, as I have previously stated, in complete ignorance of the origin of the chloride of sodium; we must consider it as one of those geological secrets upon which we shall never be able to enlighten ourselves, if we cannot obtain stronger evidence than that which we have at present. Science is at fault in this, as she is in many other subjects which have perplexed and interested from time to time those who study and seek to unravel the various obscure and complicated phenomena of nature.

No satisfactory or elucidatory theory has, as yet, been advanced to account for the occurrence of the formation of salt. Some geologists have maintained that it was deposited from the ocean, but in what way they do not explain; indeed, it is difficult to suppose how it could have been so, for salt, or rather sea water, holds in solution many ingredients which are not present in this rock. Besides, the several strata above it contain organic remains, as do also those below, though altogether of an entirely different kind;[43] rock-salt itself contains none whatever; from this fact some have inferred that the formation took place during the epoch which elapsed between the destruction of one creation and the calling of another into existence. Others suppose that it is simply the result of volcanic action: this hypothesis is correct to a certain extent, as far as isolated salt lakes like that of Tsomoriri in Western Thibet, and that lake midway between Bombay and Nagpur, are concerned; or those huge mountains consisting entirely of fossil salt, like the one near Cardona, fifty miles from Barcelona, in Spain, or those in Lahore, or in Peru; but it altogether fails as regards non-isolated salt lakes and salt marshes, or such a large inland sea as the Caspian. Some light may be thrown upon it by the recent explorations in the North-Western Provinces of India, for Mr. Wynne tells us that "the geological structure" (of the Indian Salt Range) "of the trans-Indus extension of the Salt Range repeats in a great measure that of the western portion of the Salt Range proper, but with some considerable differences. The Palœozoic rocks, so far as presented by the red-marl, rock-salt, and gypsum, are quite the same, and so are the Carboniferous and Triassic groups, but others of the sub-Carboniferous beds present themselves with a different association from those of cis-Indus." Mr. Wynne also informs us that the mineral productions of the range are valuable, and consist of the salt of Kalabagh and the Lun Nullah, the alum of Kalabagh and the Chichali Pass, the coal or lignite from the Jurassic[41] beds of the Kalabagh Hills: we also learn that gypsum is present with the salt, as it is in Poland, Transylvania, and Hungary; for in these three countries there is a layer of gypsum between the stratum of stone and the bed of salt. This gypsiferous layer is of various colours; it is crystallised, striated, and mixed with sea-shells: this admixture would decidedly lead us to conclude that the salt was originally deposited in bygone ages from the sea. On the contrary, the salt in Cheshire is not accompanied by a bed of gypsum, there are no vestiges of marine exuviæ, nor indeed any organic remains to be detected in any of the strata.

If the formation of salt (I am referring to mountains of rock-salt such as we see near Cordova, in Spain,42 and salt-mines as we see 44in Galicia, and Cheshire, and also isolated salt lakes, like that which exists in Western Thibet) is solely due to volcanic action, or marine explosion, we may easily account for its irregular and unequal distribution; also for its elevation into mountains, and as beds beneath the surface of the earth, by reason of the greater or less force which was employed for its upheaval; and also the thickness or solidity of those strata of rocks through which it was propelled in its upward course. If this were so, it is strange that it should be entirely free from organic remains, whose absence therefore is a formidable objection to this theory. Being accompanied by gypsum in some districts and not in others, would decidedly point to the presumed fact that salt has been the result of some volcanic agency; for were it not so we should find, on the contrary, owing to gradual formation, that gypsum would invariably be present with it, in the same way as we find one stratum of rock either above or below the stratum of another rock.

From the fact that deposits of salt are not confined to any particular group of strata—for while the salt-mines of Galicia belong to the tertiary formations, those in the State of New York are found in the middle of the Silurian system—we may say that salt is not subject to geological laws by reason of its somewhat erratic appearances in different strata. As the chlorides of sodium and gypsum are frequently sublimed from volcanic vents, an igneous origin has been ascribed to many of the beds of salt and gypsum; and Mr. Bakewell threw out the suggestion that the consolidation of both salt and gypsum must have been effected by heat, because the great deposit of gypsum that occurs with rock-salt at Bex, in Switzerland, was found by M. Carpentier to be anhydrous when exposed to the atmosphere. If this hypothesis is correct, and if salt and gypsum43 were at some period in a state of fusion, it is difficult to believe that when consolidated they are so perfectly distinct and in two different strata, so that one contains organic remains, whilst the other is altogether free from the slightest 45vestige. It may have been possible that one was in a state of fusion when the other was consolidated, and different degrees of heat might have been necessary for the purpose.

We also may account for the absence of organic remains in rock-salt to the following cause: the chloride of sodium, when in a state of fusion, might have possessed the property of disintegrating, dissolving, and absorbing within itself, however minute they might be, all particles of organic matter with which it came into contact. Dr. Mantell writes: "It cannot, however, be with certainty determined whether the absence or paucity of fossils in a deposit is owing to the actual reduction of the amount of life in the seas of a given area, or to the mineral character of the strata not having been favourable to the preservation of organic remains."

A very serious difficulty presents itself in the great thickness of many strata of salt; which, if regarded as the solid residuum of sea-water, must have necessarily required a proportionate volume of water, unless the seas of those distant periods contained a larger amount of saline ingredients than they do at the present time: an inference for which there are no reasonable grounds.

Wherever there are deposits of the chloride of sodium, they are almost always accompanied with layers and intercalations of gypsum; and the peculiar circumstance of two powerful acids, the sulphuric (in the gypsum, or sulphate of lime), and the muriatic or hydrochloric (in the chloride of sodium), being so abundantly and uniformly present, seems to point to a common origin; both are productions of volcanic agency, though of the two I think salt frequently owes its origin more to the subterranean activity than the gypsum, because we find there are beds of salt where there is no gypsum, and isolated salt lakes which might have been elevated into mountains had the process, during their production, been of the same force as that used in the formation of rock-salt, owing to an unexplainable interruption and premature desinence.

The relation between the formation of gypsum and volcanic action seems to be borne out by the fact that in North America, where the coal measures are not associated with rocks resulting from volcanic agency, there are no gypsum-beds; while on the contrary, there are large deposits of gypsum, where igneous rocks are interpolated beneath the stratum of coal, in Nova Scotia.44

Sir Charles Lyell, after a careful inquiry into the phenomena 46exhibited by these strata of gypsum, gives his opinion that the production of these gypsiferous beds in the carboniferous sea was closely connected with volcanic agency, whether in the form of heated vapours or stufas, or of hot mineral springs, or some other effects resulting from submarine igneous irruptions.

Salt or brine springs occur in various parts of the United States in the *old transition slate* rocks. Sir Charles Lyell tells us that, "in the middle of the horizontal Silurian rocks, in the State of New York, there is a formation of red, green, and blueish-grey marls, with beds of gypsum, and occasional salt-springs, the whole being from 800 to 1000 feet, and indistinguishable in mineral character from parts of the Trias of Europe." Salt-springs also occur in England in the coal measures. The rock-salt of Cheshire and the brine-springs of Worcestershire occur in what is called the *old red sandstone* group. The salt of Ischl, in the Austrian Alps, belongs to the *oolitic*, as does also that found in the Lias of Switzerland. The immense mass or bed of salt near Cordova occurs in the *cretaceous* group; while the salt deposit of Wieliczka belongs to the *supracretaceous* group.45

The reader doubtless remembers, as I stated in the first chapter, that the origin of salt is one of those enigmas of nature which, as yet, has completely frustrated the most accomplished and scientific geologists, and no suggestion has yet been made which will satisfactorily and conclusively account for its formation; for whatever hypothesis has been stated, there is sure to be an objection so difficult to overcome, that the author has been fain to admit that it is thoroughly impracticable, and therefore inadmissible. That it is decidedly not amenable to the received laws of geology, is apparent, which all must admit; therefore one cannot possibly apply them so as to determine the place it occupies in relation to other strata, or practically fix that period of time in which it was deposited; for it is erratic, and its position is anomalous—erratic in the variety of appearances it assumes in creation, and anomalous because it belongs to no particular strata, and therefore no exact period of time can be assigned to it as to other formations.

That salt is either due to volcanic agency, marine explosion, or to overflow of sea-water and subsequent evaporation, or resilience, and ultimate deposition, are the only three hypotheses which can with any credibility be advanced to account for its formation.

That we have it presented to us in *six* different conformations 47are facts which when considered separately seem to point to one common origin, but when taken as a whole indicate a separate inception.

Is it due to volcanic agency? In some respects it undoubtedly is, otherwise how can we reasonably account for those gigantic mountains of fossil or rock salt, which rise up isolated in the midst of a country perfectly free for miles round of saline deposits, which present not even the slightest trace of it? How can we account for it by any other means when we find it in intimate relation with gypsum, which we know is solely the production of subterranean activity? What reason can we possibly assign for those salt lakes which are above or below the sea-level and are perfectly solitary, and which have no communication with the sea or with rivers, if they are not phenomena resulting from volcanic agency? And how can we account for those masses of salt below the earth's surface which in some countries is of such adamantine hardness that it requires to be blasted with gunpowder, if it is not the production of volcanic force? If so, why is it that no remains of organic matter are found imbedded in it? How comes it, if it is the result of subterranean agency, that organic remains are found in the gypsum and none in the salt, when both are caused by volcanic explosion? Thus we see the theory of volcanic explosion is met with a most formidable objection.

If marine explosion is the sole cause of the formation of salt, and if the sea has through rents and crevices of the earth forced up its superabundant saline constituents wherever there has been a vent for their egress, and which has in the course of time become condensed owing to the evaporation of the water or through its percolating into the lower strata, another difficulty crops up quite as unanswerable seemingly as that which stands in the way of the volcanic hypothesis: there are no remains of marine organisms to be found, nor are there any traces of vegetable matter.

The overflow and evaporation of sea-water and the subsequent deposition of salt holds good in certain respects as regards salt lakes and salt marshes when they are in close proximity or in the same locality; but then those other inorganic constituents which are found as a general rule in sea-water are not present in those open reservoirs, which is a difficulty as formidable as the others, and admits of no evasion.

These are the three hypotheses with their obstacles; the hypotheses feasible, the obstacles apparently unanswerable.

48

We have salt, or the chloride of sodium, presented to us in six different conditions, viz.: *sea or salt water, salt or brine springs, salt lakes, salt mines, mountain or fossil or rock salt, and salt marshes*. The characteristics of salt are just the same fundamentally, whether we extract it by evaporation from sea-water or salt lakes; whether we obtain it from salt-springs; whether we dig it out of the earth or by the excavation of salt mountains; or whether we acquire it from salt marshes: there is no alteration in its ingredients, though it may be impure from the admixture of arsenic or the sulphates of soda and magnesia, or other impurities, or it may be discoloured red by the oxide of iron derived from decomposed trap-rocks; still, for all that, the chloride of sodium remains intact. The properties of salt are not subject to the slightest change or modification: the acid is the hydrochloric or muriatic, the base sodium, and the combination, the chloride of sodium.

We find salt, or the chloride of sodium, in sea-water, the amount averaging from 4 to 5·7 per cent., so that we see it is present in no inconsiderable quantity; it is more or less impure from other salts being held in solution in conjunction: where it comes from no suggestion has yet been broached. We know that it is present, and we also know that it can be obtained by adopting certain measures for extracting it; and we are aware, from recent investigations, that the colour and density of the sea is dependent on the quantity held in solution. This is all we really know regarding the presence of the chloride of sodium in the ocean.

The salt which we obtain from brine-springs contains the same constituents as that which we extract from the sea, though in their course upwards they collect on their way soluble salts, and therefore the water goes through certain modifications, which the reader doubtless recollects. For instance, the brine-springs of Lancashire and Worcestershire rise up through strata of sandstone and red marl, which contain large beds of rock-salt. The origin of the brine, therefore, may be derived from beds of fossil-salt; but as the muriate of soda is one of the products in volcanic regions, the original source of salt may be as deep as that of lava.46

We have also seen that the base of all mineral waters is the chloride of sodium, and that their ingredients are collected and dissolved as they ascend to the surface; therefore they may probably both have the same origin as the sea, as regards the chloride of sodium, which they both hold in solution. We can account for 49their other characteristics by the wide expansiveness of the sea, which is perpetually absorbing and emitting vapours, and by the several strata through which the mineral waters pass. There may be, though there is nothing that we can advance as corroborative, a subterranean communication existing between them, which would imply a common origin, the differences arising from the physical surroundings, atmospheric influences, and the absorption of soluble salts from the several strata.

What is the origin of salt lakes and salt marshes? This is, to a certain extent, more easily explained. One theory as to the origin of salt lakes (we naturally include inland seas, such as the Caspian and the Aral) is the overflow and subsequent retirement of the sea-water, their sites having been originally the bed of the ocean when it receded to its present limits, leaving in its course depressions of land, volumes of water of various depths, elevations, and extent of surface, according to their deepness, altitude, or angles of declivity.47 Other ingenious hypotheses have been broached, which, I need hardly say, are not worth considering, as they are entirely visionary. In the case of isolated salt lakes, the above theory is not applicable; and geologists tell us that they are doubtless the result of volcanic agency, but at what period of time it is impossible to estimate, for the density of the water found in them is not equable, and neither is their specific gravity the same as that of sea-water, nor are there any remains of marine organisms; and as their depth is variable, they are not confined to any particular strata.

I have hinted previously that these isolated salt lakes are (if I may venture to designate them as such) geological abortions. Had the power which forced them into their present situation been accompanied by that agency which has raised such huge masses as those near Cordova, in Spain, and by the Dead Sea, and which probably brought about their present crystalline form, others by reason of some unexplainable and gradual transition, by chemical means, or decrease of temperature, which naturally would occur the nearer it approached the earth's surface, these lakes might have developed into beds or mountains of salt.

50

The salt which is dug out of the earth, and that which is excavated out of isolated salt-mountains, are alike in every respect, and are much more probably the result of volcanic explosion than of the deposition of salt from sea-water, accruing from evaporation while pent up in confined spaces. It may have been, though incalculable ages ago, deposited from the sea, and then in course of time forced up while in a state of fusion by some internal disruption.

We thus see that the six conditions under which we find the chloride of sodium more or less indicate a common origin from sea-water, notwithstanding the absence of marine organisms.

If we take salt as a whole, leaving out of the question altogether the different conditions in which it is found, and with no reference at all to its existing either in the earth, above the earth, in lakes, or in the sea, but looking at it simply as it is, a mass of rock, or a volume of water holding it in solution, it inclines one to the belief that it possesses a dual inchoation, though the original source of both may have been connate; but owing to extraneous causes which were brought to bear, one branch became crystallised rock-salt, while the other, through immaturity, remains in a state of solution. One is rock-salt, which has been heaved up by volcanic power, and the other is what is known as sea-water; the former has produced the mines, and the solitary mountains, and the Indian Salt Range, and that salt which generates mineral waters, and, it may be, those saline lakes like that which exists between Bombay and Nagpur.

According to Sir Charles Lyell, sea-water has access to volcanic foci. He says: "Although the theory which assumes that water plays a principal part in volcanic operations does not necessarily imply the proximity of volcanic vents to the ocean, it seems still to follow naturally that the superficial outbursts of steam and lava will be most prevalent where there is an incumbent body of salt water, or any regions rather than in the interior of a continent, where the quantity of rain-water is reduced to a minimum. The experiments of the most eminent chemists have gradually removed, one after another, the objections which were first offered to the doctrine that the salt water of the sea plays a leading part in most volcanic eruptions. Sir Humphry Davy observed that the fumes which escaped from Vesuvian lava deposited common salt."

All the principal volcanoes are situated close to the sea, and 51 therefore the hypothesis that a communication exists between them is practically certain; their proximity to the sea, and the deposition of salt from the fumes of lava, as Sir Humphry Davy noticed, are two strong facts. But for all that, it does not prove satisfactorily that salt is solely the result of volcanic agency, and indirectly from the sea, because there is not the slightest trace of the remains of marine organisms, unless they are totally destroyed and obliterated when it is in a state of fusion; if so, it is more conclusive that salt such as we find it is solely due to volcanic force. Salt may have been in times past, as the observations of Sir Humphry Davy seem to corroborate, and as confirmed by more recent chemists, deposited by volcanic agency in the same way that salt is deposited by fumes of hydrochloric acid, which are emitted with the lava during eruptions of such volcanoes as Vesuvius and Etna, by reason of some communication with the sea.

As hydrochloric acid is found in the vapours which are disengaged from red-hot lava, and as magnesia, which is not volatile, is left in the lava itself, constituting one of its most important elements, it would certainly lead one to surmise that there is a communication which, though not always in existence, may be periodically caused by the action of the volcano.

Both MM. St. Claire Deville and Fouqué have succeeded in demonstrating the perfect accordance of the chemical composition of the products of volcanic eruptions, both gaseous and solid, with the doctrine that salt water has been largely present in volcanic foci. If so, why are there no salts of magnesia in volcanic fumeroles? These salts are readily decomposable by hot steam, and when water and heat are present they produce hydrochloric acid and magnesia. M. Fouqué affirmed that he witnessed an eruption of Mount Etna in 1865; the gaseous emanations agreed in kind with those which we might have looked for if large volumes of sea-water had gained access to reservoirs of subterranean lava, and if they had been decomposed and expelled with the lava.48 We have obtained three facts, viz., that communications probably exist between volcanic foci and sea-water; that fumes of hydrochloric acid which accompany the lava deposit common salt; and that the salts of magnesia are decomposed by heat; and what more probable than that all living organisms which pass with the sea-water are utterly obliterated?

By the preceding observations, the reader will see that salt is not 52subject to geological laws, by reason of its being confined to no particular strata, and by the absence of organic remains; and that it is not derived from sea-water, because there are no marine organisms to be found in it.

That though it may have a pristine source, it has (though it may appear paradoxical) a dual inchoation—by its being found as rock-salt, and by its being present in sea-water, and, as I have stated, in a condition of immaturity.

Rock-salt appears to be the result of volcanic agency, from its being almost invariably (with but few exceptions) in juxtaposition with gypsum, which is known to be of volcanic origin; by its being found forced up independently of other formations, even through the crust of the earth; by the presence of fumes of hydrochloric acid with lava during volcanic eruptions.

It has undoubtedly an igneous origin, and the entire absence of organic remains may be accounted for by the fact that while in a state of fusion it may have disintegrated, absorbed into itself, or altogether obliterated all remains of living organisms with which it may have come into immediate contact. All other formations have preserved the impress and structure of vegetable and animal life; salt is the sole exception to the rule; and if while in a state of fusion it possessed the property of destroying and obliterating all marks of animal and vegetable remains, we can easily account for their absence.49

We have also seen that sea-water has access to volcanic foci, by reason of fumes of hydrochloric acid, which deposit common salt, and by the proximity of the volcanoes to the sea.

One question is naturally evolved out of this: does the sea obtain its saline constituents from vast reservoirs, or beds of salt, through the medium of communication with volcanic foci?

This question I leave unsolved, for were we to discuss it, we should probably have to enter into other matters which would be somewhat foreign to my subject. My opinion is that sea-water (if my hypothesis that it is nothing else than salt in a state of immaturity is correct) obtains its chloride of sodium in this way; and, if so, it accounts at once for the absence of marine organisms, upon which phenomenon geologists have always laid so much stress. 53 Besides, if salt is derived from evaporation of sea-water, and subsequent deposition of salt, we should be able to obtain remains of marine organisms, if not those of land animals. This one fact alone would tend to prove that sea-water is the result of some subterranean communication with reservoirs of salt, through the media of volcanic foci.

We have thus before us certain geological facts relative to salt, which show that though it has not been discovered in the old stratified rocks, it is nevertheless met with in nearly all the later formations, and also that it is in process of formation, and notably so in the Crimea. This undoubtedly is the case; but still we cannot apply any of the laws of geology so as to make our conjectures confirmative by certain facts which support one hypothesis and overthrow another.

CHAPTER VI.

EFFECTS ON ANIMAL AND VEGETABLE LIFE.

As salt is one of the principal constituents of the blood, and as it is present in the various tissues of the body, and as its ingestion is necessary for the animal economy, for the maintenance of its health, and consequently for the due development of the several organs, and the invigorating effects it exerts over their functional activity, we will now consider it in the relation it holds to animal and vegetable life.

By the great majority of land animals salt is evidently an article much relished, for in those districts where salt springs and lakes are prevalent, many quadrupeds and birds are invariably to be seen.[50] They frequent these spots in great numbers, and very seldom migrate to those districts which are deficient in salt, or, if they do, very speedily return; these animal instincts are indicative that they are aware of its bracing qualities, and experience the salubriousness of the atmosphere, which naturally is impregnated with a fair amount of salt, which has risen through the media of exhalations from the water or evaporation of the same.

In the Ruminantia the beneficial and, indeed, the salutary action of salt is remarkably observable, for it counteracts in this class of animals the deleterious effects of rainy weather, damp pasturage, 54and damaged fodder. It also imparts a consistency to the fat, and renders the meat more palatable and wholesome. All cattle, without an exception, thrive best if they are supplied with salt; and they will consume no small quantity. Horses will, on the average, consume daily six ounces; cows, four ounces, and will, it is said, secrete a larger quantity of milk, and of a much richer quality, than those from which salt is usually withheld. Sheep will consume half an ounce daily, and they are not affected with the rot, as is so frequently the case in low-lying marshy districts where they drink water in which there are myriads of the fluke-worm, embryonic and developed, especially after heavy rains or inundations, as, for instance, a river overflowing its banks. It is a fact which farmers and graziers should by no means lose sight of, that these worms are totally destroyed by giving sheep a certain amount of salt during moist and wet seasons, and in those localities which are generally in a state of humidity.

In marine animals common salt is a necessary constituent of their drink, and in fact it is the preserver of their life; but it is injurious, if not certain destruction, to many fresh-water fish, though some live both in the sea and fresh water—as the salmon, sturgeon, and some species of lamprey. The male salmon, on entering the mouths of rivers in order to spawn, follow the females, and fecundate the ova which they have deposited in little pools, or kinds of nests. They, therefore, are hatched in rivers. After the first year they remove to the sea, and, remaining in it for about two months to ten weeks, return to fresh water. Such is the alternate fresh and salt-water life of the salmon, showing us that some fish can live in the sea and breed in fresh water.

Reptiles and animals of an inferior class are deprived of life by the action of salt water; and such organisms as the amœba, hydra, rotifer, and others of a similar grade which we see in stagnant ponds, are speedily killed if put into water in which salt is dissolved; this is also the case with earth-worms, snails, and indeed all insects as a general rule, especially if generated by animal and vegetable decay.

Owing to the antagonism of salt to life produced by putrefaction, it is frequently rubbed into meat to prevent it from being attacked by putrescent larvæ; and even if decomposition has commenced, it arrests for a long time its further progress. We all know what an intense irritant it is to leeches, and how they immediately vomit if some salt is sprinkled upon them when they are engorged with blood.

Land shells are rapidly killed by sea-water, and so are their eggs; this fact has been demonstrated by Darwin, who says: "Their eggs, at least such as I have tried, sink into it and are killed." From experiments performed by Baron Aucapitaine, we find the above corroborated. He placed in a box, pierced with holes, one hundred land shells belonging to ten different species, and then immersed it in sea-water for a fortnight; *only* twenty-seven recovered.

These experiments are conclusive, and prove that salt destroys life of an inferior grade, probably owing to the fact that, generally, it is calculated to produce results of a nature somewhat disposed to become an annoyance, or even inimical to the vitalisation of superior organisms, and tends to arrest their progress and due development. We must remember that these two experiments of Mr. Darwin and Baron Aucapitaine were with sea-water, consequently the other salts which it holds in solution (the sulphates of soda and magnesia), and the organic matter which it contains, very probably hastened the progress.

The Batrachians, a class of animals allied to the reptiles, but undergoing a peculiar metamorphosis, have an antipathy to salt, and consequently cannot live in salt water; it is death to them sooner or later.

We cannot say that reptiles, as a rule, frequent fresh water in preference to salt, some being found only in sea-water, and in those parts of the ocean where there is a greater quantity of saline matter than in others. There is the marine Chelonia, for instance, commonly known as turtles (Chelones); one sub-group, the common green turtle, so well known for its palatable qualities, is composed of species altogether herbivorous, and of gregarious and innocent habits, "These animals may be seen in herds at the bottom of the sea, quietly browsing on the weeds growing there. Sometimes they enter the mouths of large rivers, and are occasionally seen to make their way ashore, apparently in search of food."[51] Like the salmon, it is a habitat of both fresh and sea water, though under different conditions; one frequents fresh-water for food, the other for breeding. Another sub-group comprises turtles of carnivorous habits, active, and, when attacked, fierce; such is the loggerhead turtle and the hawksbill; the latter is the animal which furnishes the arts with the elegant substance called tortoise-shell. There is also a genus of carnivorous habits, called the Sphargis, or coriaceous turtle.

There are likewise the river tortoises (Tryonices), which are conspicuous tenants of the Ganges, the Euphrates, the Niger, the Nile, the Mississippi, and the Ohio. These reptiles are next in size to the turtles, some being three feet long; they are very fierce, and do not even scruple to attack the young alligators. They live principally on fresh-water fish and small reptiles; sometimes they will venture into sea-water in quest of food, though not far, as we may suppose. There are also the Emydes, which are sometimes called fresh-water tortoises, sometimes marsh tortoises, which are of many different species. They haunt lakes, marshes, and small rivers in Asia, Africa, and Australia, but more particularly America, where the proper habitat is represented. In the North American rivers there is found the Emysaura serpentina, which has a large head and crocodilian tail; it feeds on fishes and small birds. Another species, called Chelys fimbriata, or Matamata, belongs exclusively to the rivers of Guiana.

We thus see that the Chelonia, which are remarkable for the box-like case in which most of them are enclosed, are inhabitants of the sea, while their near relations, the tortoises, are only partially aquatic in their habits.

Reptiles are therefore neither land, sea-water, nor fresh-water animals, if we view them as a whole; but if we divide them into orders, we shall be able to see at once which are fresh-water, which are terrestrial, and which are inhabitants proper of the sea. Firstly, there is the Amphibia (doubled-lived), which live and breed in fresh water, such as rivers, lakes, ponds, and ditches, and which are killed if put into salt water. Secondly, there is the Ophidia (snake-like order), which are peculiar to the land, though there is a fresh-water snake in the East Indies, and which the natives will boldly attack with sticks. The Sauria (lizards) next claim our attention. The alligator is a native of North America, and is very abundant in the Mississippi. It is very seldom seen near the mouths of rivers, and in winter it buries itself in the mud, and continues in a torpid state till spring. Then there are the crocodiles, which are natives of Africa, the West Indies, and America. Their habits are somewhat similar to those of the alligator, frequenting the creeks of rivers by night in search of food; they are sometimes seen near the mouths of rivers, but not as a rule. We have already remarked upon the Testudinata, or the turtle kind.

Reptiles, therefore, either frequent the land or the water; some are purely aquatic, others purely terrestrial, the remainder are both;57 one order is altogether marine, though frequently they are seen on shore, where they are caught.

Salt water is death to one order, but affords the means of life to another; to yet another order, with but few exceptions, both salt and fresh water are deleterious, and, in fact, death; whilst still another order frequents both elements, just as the chances of obtaining food may direct them.

Such animals as the hippopotamus, the rhinoceros, the tapir, and the elephant, and a few others belonging to the Pachydermata, frequent the banks of rivers and fresh-water lakes, where they wallow in the mud, and now and then, as fancy takes them, splash about in the water; but they, like the crocodile, have never been known, as far as I can gather, to make for salt water, and therefore they are seldom, if ever, seen near the mouths of rivers, or by the coast.

Salt is therefore not avoided, almost as a rule, either by animals or birds; and in those districts where salt lakes are situated (to which interesting fact I have already alluded) are to be invariably seen, not only great numbers of animals, but large flocks of birds of different kinds, showing conclusively that they possess an instinctive preference for those localities where the atmosphere is more or less filled with saline matter, than for those places where it is entirely absent. It is but seldom that animals frequent those spots which are injurious to them; they take good care to avoid them, if possible, and if they detect anything deleterious, whether it be in the air, soil, or water, they migrate to more genial quarters; instinct indicates this necessity, and they accordingly act upon it. It is strange that mere animal instinct should be superior to human reason, and that animal sagacity should be more far-seeing than human forethought! Nothing is more strongly confirmative of this anomaly, if I may call it so, than the partiality which animals entertain for those districts which abound with salt lakes, and the antipathy, or utter indifference, with which some people regard that substance which keeps the body pure, healthy, and, I may say, clean, and which plays such a highly-important part in the animal economy.

In the vegetable kingdom salt is by no means an inconsiderable item, and as an agricultural agent it is most invaluable, though its operation therein varies in a remarkable degree; in small quantities it is injurious only to a few plants, while to some it appears to be beneficial in every way. In moderation it is an excellent manure, especially if the soil is of a sandy nature; but in large quantities58 it is decidedly pernicious to all plants, without an exception, though unequally so. According to experiments made by Dr. Balfour and other eminent botanists, it appears that a solution of the chloride of sodium does not act so deleteriously as solutions of other inorganic substances, and the same effect is observable with a solution of the phosphate of soda: the strength of these solutions, we are told, varied from half a grain to five grains to the ounce of water; the sodium combined with the chlorine forming the chloride of sodium, and with the oxygen forming soda; the potassium, combined with the chlorine, forming the chloride of potassium, and with the oxygen forming potassa. The combinations take place, according to Johnston, in the living plants owing to the natural affinities of these inorganic substances.

Darwin writes: "In botanical works, this or that plant is often stated to be ill-adapted for wide dissemination, but the greater or less facilities for transport across the sea may be said to be almost wholly unknown. Until I tried, with Mr. Berkeley's aid, a few experiments, it was not even known how far seeds could resist the injurious action of sea-water. To my surprise I found that out of 87 kinds, 64 germinated after an immersion of 28 days, and a few survived an immersion of 137 days. It deserves notice that certain orders were far more injured than others; nine Leguminosæ were tried, and, with one exception, they resisted the salt-water badly; seven species of the allied orders, Hydrophyllaceæ and Polemoniaceæ, were all killed by a month's immersion. For convenience' sake, I chiefly tried small seeds, without the capsules or fruit; and as all these sank in a few days, they could not have been floated across wide spaces of the sea, whether or not they were injured by the salt-water. Afterwards I tried some larger fruits, capsules, etc., and some of these floated for a long time. It is well known what a difference there is in the buoyancy of green and seasoned timber; and it occurred to me that floods would often wash into the sea dried plants or branches with seed capsules or fruit attached to them. Hence I was led to dry the stems and branches of 94 plants with ripe fruit, and to place them on sea-water. The majority sank quickly, but some which, whilst green, floated for a very short time, when dried floated much longer; for instance, ripe hazel-nuts sank immediately, but when dried they floated for 90 days, and afterwards when planted germinated; an asparagus-plant with ripe berries floated for 23 days, when dried it floated for 85 days, and the seeds afterwards germinated; the ripe seeds of Helosciadium59 sank in 2 days, when dried they floated for above 90 days, and afterwards germinated. Altogether, out of the 94 dried plants, 18 floated for above 28 days; and some of the 18 floated for a very much longer period. So that as 64/87 kinds of seeds germinated after an immersion of 28 days; and as 18/94 distinct species with ripe fruit (but not all the same species, as in the foregoing experiment) floated, after being dried, for above 28 days, we may conclude, as far as anything can be inferred from these scanty facts, that the seeds of 14/100 kinds of plants of any country might be floated by sea-currents during 28 days and would retain their power of germination."

We have thus sufficient evidence before us to prove that salt or sea water does not totally destroy the vitality of seeds when they are in a dry state, that some of them will float for 90 days, and when planted subsequently will germinate; but that when not dry they will sink immediately. We may, therefore, justly conclude from the result of these experiments that salt is not noxious to vegetable life, neither does it destroy the latent principle of procreation which exists in them; and that though the process of germination may be retarded, and kept in a state of abeyance, it is not virtually annihilated, as one would feel inclined to predict, by the prolonged immersion of seeds in salt-water, be they dried or fresh.

Darwin's experiments were afterwards verified, for he states that subsequently M. Martens tried "similar ones, but in a much better manner, for he placed the seeds in a box in the actual sea, so that they were alternately wet and exposed to the air like really floating plants. He tried 98 seeds, mostly different from mine; but he chose many large fruits and likewise seeds from plants which live near the sea; and this would have favoured both the average length of their flotation, and their resistance to the injurious action of the salt water. On the other hand, he did not previously dry the plants or branches with the fruit; and this, as we have seen, would have caused some of them to have floated much longer. The result was that 18/98 of his seeds of different kinds floated for 42 days, and were then capable of germination. But I do not doubt that plants exposed to the waves would float for a less time than those protected from violent movement as in our experiments. Therefore it would, perhaps, be safe to assume that the seeds of about 10/100 parts of a flora, after having been dried, could be floated across a space of 900 miles in width, and would then germinate. The fact of the larger fruits often floating longer than the small, is interesting; as plants with large seeds or fruit which, as Alph. de Candolle has shown, 60 generally have restricted ranges, could hardly be transported by other means."

Darwin's experiments show us that salt or sea water does not entirely extirpate the life which is dormant in seeds, and those of Martens prove that seeds may be immersed in sea-water itself and yet retain the power of germination; and that when dry they may even float for 900 miles, and germinate when planted; developing into plants at the usual period of time allotted by nature!

In Cheshire it is a custom to let out the water of the salt-springs after rain, in order to improve the character of the soil and make it more productive. If we call to mind the preservative properties of salt and the purifying action which it possesses, with regard to animal and vegetable substances, we need not at all be surprised at the above use to which it is put by the agriculturists of Cheshire. The reader, perhaps, would like to know why it is used after rain. After a heavy shower, and more especially in the country, every insect leaves its little secluded habitation: the bee is once more on the wing; the spider resumes his usual central position in his web; flies of all sizes buzz here and there in search of food or for more secure homes; every bush is alive with its usual occupants; the lofty tree is once more the tenement of song; the caterpillar crawls on his solitary way; the ant trudges along on the gravel-path; the snail emerges from his retreat and plods slowly to another home; and the earth-worm raises itself on the lawn; all with one accord hail the reappearance of sunshine, and show signs, however feeble, of joy that the rain-cloud has passed and that the landscape has resumed its beauties, and the sky its gold and azure. The earth after rain, and particularly in spring and summer, teems with almost reanimated life, both with that which is harmless and with that which is hurtful, so that the Cheshire custom is one which cannot be too highly recommended, for when the soil is saturated with moisture, a soluble salt like the chloride of sodium, already in a state of solution, sinks in more rapidly, and permeates it more thoroughly than if it were merely sprinkled over the surface; and such insects as are associated with or which live in the earth are speedily eliminated, or are forced to seek shelter at a greater depth, where they ultimately die by reason of their inability to obtain their proper sustenance or the unsuitableness of their new abode.

There is a plant called Halimodendron which only grows in the dry, naked salt-fields by the river Irtysh, in Siberia; it is a genus61 of the Leguminosæ, and has purple flowers. Saltwort, or Salsola, (*salsus*, salt) is chiefly maritime, and the kelp of our shores is principally obtained from it. At one time the carbonate of soda was derived from this kelp or barilla, the ashes being obtained from burning sea-weeds and a species of Salsola; but now it is almost invariably made from common salt, by adding sulphuric acid, and so converting the chloride of sodium into a sulphate, and afterwards, by combustion with chalk and small coal, resolving it into a sulphide, and then into a carbonate. It is manufactured on a very large scale, and is an important staple of commerce. From it is obtained a most important drug, the bicarbonate of soda, the efficacy of which everyone, more or less, has once in a lifetime experienced.

This kelp has been put to a fraudulent use, for Sir Robert Christison tells us that disease has been traced to an impure kind of salt, in which, when investigated, the hydriodate of soda was detected, resulting, he says, from an inferior salt obtained from kelp.52

In all those districts which are intersected by salt marshes, there is almost a complete absence of miasmatic effluvia, though, as a natural consequence, the vegetation is not of that rank luxuriance which is invariably to be seen in other marsh lands; because, whenever the soil is in a state of moisture, it is always covered with all kinds of weeds and useless plants, which altogether stop the growth of those which are of utility to the agriculturist.

In the case of salt marshes it is the reverse, and the neighbourhood is perfectly free from those endemic diseases which are prevalent in such localities as the fen-country, and other similar districts; for the atmosphere is pure, and the soil comparatively dry, and intermittent fever is unknown.

CHAPTER VII.

MEDICINAL AND DIETETIC PROPERTIES.

Salt, except by the ignorant, is generally acknowledged to be a condiment, not only requisite as an adjunct to food, but also for the animal economy; this fact is not to be lost sight of, and therefore I lay much stress on it, and in the next chapter we shall see 62that physiologically it holds no mean position amongst those other substances which are found in the human body.

There are a number of facts of physiological import, at which it is necessary to glance, and which are indissolubly connected with its medicinal and dietetic properties; and there are various others illustrative of the absolute necessity of salt, which are self-evident to those who think and observe, and which we will now proceed to lay before the reader.

In human blood, salt is a most important constituent; where there is disease, there is a diminution of salt, with corresponding nervous depression, and the individual experiences a want of power: if this want continues for any length of time, the health is gradually undermined; the blood loses its richness and is deprived of its vitalising property; various symptoms finally show themselves, and probably develop into some phenomena of a serious significance—all, indeed, indicative that the system is deficient of a most important essential in its economy. These symptoms may prognosticate the approach of various diseased conditions, partly owing to the habits, constitution, or surroundings of the patient. In all morbid conditions, and particularly in those which owe their origin to an unhealthy state of the blood, we may, to a considerable extent, be certain that there is a deficiency of the chloride of sodium. In proof of this, patients never, as a rule, object to salt; they actually relish it. Why? Because there is a deficiency, and nature intuitively excites the desire. We often find that patients refuse sugar; indeed the very mention of it produces a feeling of nausea and extreme disgust: with salt it is entirely different; they take it, and, in most cases, enjoy it in the same way that fever-stricken patients long for, and relish, a draught of cold water, *if* they are able to obtain it.

Were the human race once deprived of the chloride of sodium, even for a limited period of time, we should not only lose a natural healthful incentive for our food, but disease, with all her attendant miseries, would spread with such relentless impetuosity as would defy, and even paralyse, the efforts of the most skillful physician, the ingenuity of the surgeon, and the scientific improvements and hygienic precautions of the sanitarian.53 The strength and vigour of manhood would fade as if blasted by disease, food would act as a poison; the blood would not be replenished with the salt which 63it requires, and consequently our skins would soon be covered with corruption; our cattle would die, our crops would be nipped in the bud; the air would be full of offensive insects; the soil would become foul and barren, the sea a waste of stagnant waters; and all the beautiful productions of nature would wither and decay, and our glorious earth would degenerate into a hideous solitude, solely inhabited, very probably, by monsters horrible to behold, and more repulsive than those gigantic reptiles which once roamed by the dreary marshes of an incomplete world.

Those who take pleasure in decrying the inimitable works of nature, and affirm that they are provocative of evil, can only support their arguments by brazen assertions and subtle paralogisms.

Common salt is considered by most persons as a mere luxury, as if its use were only to gratify the taste, although it is essential to health and life, and is indeed as much an aliment or food as either bread or flesh. It is a constituent of most of our food and drinks, and nature has kindly furnished us with an appetite for it, though there are not a few who regard it quite in another light: that quadrupeds and birds (as I have before stated) should be fully alive to the vivifying properties of salt, and that mankind should be indifferent to, and in many instances totally ignorant of them, is somewhat curious and incomprehensible, but it is so.

Another strange fact is, that savage nations use it freely with but few exceptions: on the other hand, in civilised life there are a great number who never touch it; but these abstainers little think that they carry in their countenances visible signs of ill-health, and their impurity of skin indicates that at some future time disease, in some form or other, will cause them to regret, in more ways than one, that their short-sighted neglect has prepared a soil ready to receive the seeds of some fever, and other maladies more deadly and obstinate.

Cutaneous eruptions, so distressing to the patient, and so disgusting to an observer, flourish when they attack those who have abstained from the use of salt.

Everyone perspires or sweats: the indolent perspire, the laborious sweat. This distinction will be regarded as too fine by those who entertain the opinion that perspiration and sweat mean the same thing; this, however, is a great error; there is a marked difference between perspiring and sweating, as much difference, indeed, between these two processes of the elimination of refuse animal matter, as there is between walking and running. It is true64 the same laws of nature are brought into play; but one is a modification of the other. Those of a spare habit are seldom in a state of general diaphoresis, and are only so when the weather is sultry, or when they have taken a walk on a hot summer's day. The stout or plethoric, on the contrary, sweat copiously, even on the slightest movement; and it is really a good thing for them that they do, for otherwise they would very likely be attacked with a fit of apoplexy, or would fall down from syncope; the former arising from the flow of too much blood to the brain, or from rupture of an artery; the latter resulting from an insufficient supply; or the blood owing to its circulating in an impure state, which is practically the case if there is a deficiency of salt, would generate, not what is generally considered disease, but a condition which would render the system prepared for the reception and development of morbific influences.

During perspiration the blood is deprived, in proportion as the diaphoresis continues, not only of the liquor-sanguinis, but of the chloride of sodium which it holds in solution. Though to a certain extent perspiration is an act of nature necessary for the continuance of health, yet, if it goes beyond a point which is consistent with an equalisation of the several secretions, the individual experiences a diminution or loss of power, and nervous exhaustion or irritability is the result. In natural diaphoresis the only way in which the system can recuperate itself is by quenching the thirst; for free perspiration is generally or almost invariably succeeded by a corresponding thirst, varying in intensity according to the peculiar idiosyncrasy of the individual.

Thin people do not perspire so copiously as those who are more stoutly built, therefore they do not lose so much and neither do they require so much fluid. Their blood, by reason of its retaining its liquor-sanguinis and its chloride of sodium, does not require salt as an aliment so freely as those who, owing to their profuse perspiration, are in constant want of it. Stout people, or those who have a superabundance of adipose tissue (for I must observe there is a great difference between stoutness and obesity, though in common parlance the two words are synonymous), require salt in a greater degree than thin people. Well-developed muscles covering a well-made frame, accompanied by a proper and due proportion of fat, constitute stoutness of a healthy standard; but small muscles covered with an overdue amount of fat, with an abdomen distended to an offensive size (which is so frequently seen), seem, in my65 opinion, to determine a habit of a Vitellian obesity, if I may so apply the name of that Roman epicure.

Owing to the fact that stout and fat people perspire freely and profusely, and to a much greater extent when undergoing fatigue, they must necessarily lose a great amount of salt; for as it is held in solution by the liquor-sanguinis, which passes through the pores of the skin in the form of sweat (the word perspiration is not sufficiently emphatic when we are speaking of stout and fat individuals), it must naturally pass out with it, and thus they experience thirst and a desire for salt; which desire is strongly indicative of a healthy state of the secretions. If there is no wish for salt, then we may conclude that disease in some form or other is lurking unsuspected in the system, ready to break out, either by an act of indiscretion, poisoned atmosphere, or because of a taint of an hereditary character. We may compare this condition of things to a barrel of gunpowder, ready on the application of the faintest spark to ignite, and spread confusion and death far and wide, with a fury proportionate to the amount of the inflammatory material. If these people do not take salt with their food they allow their blood to become impoverished and more unhealthy than it already is, and their constitutions materially suffer in consequence, their skins are ultimately affected, the complexion frequently becomes sallow, and appears discoloured, and in some severe cases we have that skin disease called acnæ, indicative of the poor and unwholesome state of the blood; they are affected with intestinal parasites, they do not digest their food, their breath has a most disagreeable odour, very unmistakable, and they are more or less out of health.

Those of a scrofulous habit require salt to a much greater extent than even the gross, because the blood of scrofulous or strumous persons does not possess its due proportion of salt; and the only way to make up for this deficiency is to use it freely, otherwise the system does not derive the support and nourishment from that source which vitalises the whole frame. We may justly infer that if the blood is deficient of a most important constituent the system must, as a matter of course, degenerate into a condition not only ready to receive disease, but into one which reduces the strength and undermines the nerve-power, and this in a scrofulous habit is fraught with serious consequences.

The chronic inflammation which attacks the joints in scrofula sometimes occurs, not so much from the unhealthy low state of the system, but rather from the impure condition of the blood, result66ing from the partial absence of salt. This must be the case, because the sufferer experiences an increased vitality if salt is used more abundantly; the change of course is gradual, and therefore we must not expect to see one's efforts immediately crowned with success. It is sometimes necessary to explain to scrofulous patients the unhealthiness of a persistent avoidance of salt, and to point out to them the benefits accruing from it, and also to insist upon their using it, because, owing to their ignorance of its operation and their unwise dislike, they look upon it in the light of a noxious compound.

I have frequently noticed (and I dare say others have observed the same thing) the disfiguring eruptions with which many people (and especially the young) of a scrofulous habit, and even some who are free from this taint, are afflicted about the face and neck. These pimples and blotches, when not caused by constipation, are generally accompanied by a swollen condition of the glands, which are sometimes acutely sensitive to the slightest pressure.

If we were to question them closely we should find that salt is to them an almost unknown article of diet, or distasteful to them, though no doubt it is, in some few instances, used but sparingly and seldom.

The blood, more or less, is always undergoing a change, even in health; the nitrogenised and non-nitrogenised substances are invariably variable, and at no two moments are the salts of the same proportion, its alkalescence always being in a constant state of variation. Notwithstanding our increased facilities for obtaining a better acquaintance with disease than formerly, the few facts which have been satisfactorily made out show us that as yet we have made but little progress as regards the morbid conditions of the human blood, and that a great deal remains to be accomplished before we are masters of the subject.

Amongst the chief diseases in which a pathognomonic condition of the blood has been discovered is the increase of the fibrine, which always takes place in inflammatory diseases, such as acute rheumatism and inflammation of the lungs; in low fevers it is diminished; it is also subject to variation in other diseases. In typhoid fever the diminution of salt and the increase of fibrine is very marked; and indeed in all inflammatory states of the system, especially of a sthenic type, the partial absence or variation of the amount of the chloride of sodium is a most important characteristic. No attention has, up to the present time, been given to the relation which the67 presence of the chloride of sodium in the blood bears to disease, at least not that I am aware of; and from what I have noticed it opens up a question which in time will be considered of some moment. As the chloride of sodium obviates the tendency of the fibrine to coagulate, and as its coagulation or solubility is quite dependent on its normal amount in the blood, it presents to us many varied points of interest, not only physiologically, but medicinally, though in this respect it has not yet been recognised as a curative agent.

Whenever the blood is impoverished we may be tolerably certain that salt is, in a greater or lesser degree, absent, or below the standard, and that it is variable.

Now in scrofula the blood is not only vitiated, but poor in the extreme, and there is a decrease of the fibrine; and that being the case, the constitution suffers in proportion, the affection showing itself in various ways, which unmistakably indicate the adynamic state of that fluid which permeates the whole frame.

Scrofula and her twin sister struma, for there is a difference, are low forms of chronic inflammatory cachexia, and are never entirely recovered from. We may justly term them systemic diseases originating local morbid phenomena, and which are always liable to give rise to obscure attacks of an apparently serious nature, but which are considerably modified if the treatment be simply hygienic, judicious, and practical; scrofula is always tedious and prolonged, and therefore, as I have said before, we must not anticipate that because salt is of a nature somewhat antidotal to it and its attendant evils, that its effects are to be observable instantaneously, or that any very remarkable results must necessarily be obtained. It is the reverse; the effects are slow in the extreme, but the benefit is permanent—that is, if the treatment adopted be calculated to restore to the blood that constituent so necessary for health.

This is easily explained—the unhealthiness of the system arising from mal-nutrition, owing to the blood being more or less deficient of a constituent which is necessary for the promotion of health, and being solely constitutional, it takes some time to make up for that deficiency, and to supply that which is lost. A disease of long standing, and of an hereditary character, is not speedily recovered from, particularly if the mischief is caused by, or is dependent upon, an impure state of the blood, and if there is not the normal amount of the chloride of sodium it must of necessity be corrupt.

68

Though salted provisions are apt to produce scurvy if continued for too long a time, yet in the case of those on board ship I do not think it arises exclusively from the salt itself, but by the unwholesome food upon which the toilers of the sea are obliged too often to subsist. The biscuits, which are of the coarsest kind, and sometimes worm-eaten, are certainly not calculated to keep up the stamina of the men; and the salt pork which they have three or four times a week is not exactly the food to promote a healthy condition of the blood; neither is the soup, which is little better than rice water, capable of even satisfying the cravings of hunger.

Besides, there is a very miserable custom, and which tends to ruin the health of our sailors, and that is the drink which is, I may say, encouraged on board ship, and officially served out to them daily, in the shape of rum, though of late they can have cocoa if they prefer. So habituated have they become to this that no captain would think of suggesting a diminution of the supply. Our sailors, poor fellows! will stand anything but the deprivation of their "grog;" they do not mind being crowded like beasts of burden in a close, stifling forecastle, eating coarse biscuits or unwholesome pickled pork, so long as they are duly supplied with their "grog" and allowed to go "ashore" and spend their contemptible pittance on poisonous compounds which burn their stomachs and sow the seeds of some deadly disease, and especially if they happen to be in the tropics.

All these inseparable accompaniments of nautical life are, without doubt, provocative of scurvy to a certain extent, and I am sure do not help to stave it off. If rum is taken on an empty stomach, day after day, as regularly as clockwork, we cannot expect that the men should be in a state of sound health, or that their blood should be pure; particularly if the voyage is long, the biscuits worm-eaten, the pickled pork of a questionable condition, sometimes even approaching putridity, and the rice-soup—upon which I shall abstain from passing any remarks, further than by saying that it is decidedly not of that quality tending to act as a substantial sustentation of men who work hard, and who are exposed to all weathers, both by night and by day. Indeed it is surprising that they can perform their duties as they do when we call to mind their irregularities, their daily use of spirits, and their periodical alcoholic indulgences when ashore, combined with their abominable diet on board ship.

Though salted provisions solely are not altogether conducive to69 health, or contributive towards preserving the due equalisation of the constituents of the blood, I cannot see that they entirely originate scurvy, as some assert; I am of an opinion that this disease is caused principally by seamen's peculiar habits, and the surroundings belonging to a seafaring life, joined, much more frequently than some would like to confess, with the ingestion of animal food just rescued from putrescence by a timely immersion in brine.

Everything, as is well known, can be used and abused, and salt, like other natural productions, owing to human avarice, can be put to a purpose so as to derange and render nugatory the laws of health. We know full well that salt completely arrests the formation of putrescent larvæ in meat, if it is rubbed in when fresh, or if it is well soaked in strong brine; and if the meat is bordering on decomposition, we may prevent it proceeding to a more advanced stage by immersing it in brine; still it is not in a condition fit for human consumption. Such food in my opinion is of a nature calculated to produce disease of a most virulent type; indeed it is quite sufficient to produce the worse form of scurvy, let alone the outbreaks of a milder degree.

I am acquainted with the fact that a diet consisting exclusively of salt pork and salt beef, with very little variation or change, would be, if continued for any length of time, combined with the absence of fresh vegetables, productive of much mischief, and in the end no doubt scurvy would be the result; but for us to assert that every outbreak of this disease is produced by salted provisions, is to run into a very ridiculous error, and we fall into a trap cunningly laid for us by those whose interest it is to keep up this preposterous imposition in the eyes of the not too discerning public. If shipowners took more care in provisioning their ships with wholesome food, instead of allowing them to be stored with bad pork, putrid beef, and rotten biscuits, we should not read the heart-sickening accounts so frequently in the newspapers. It is all very well for them to assert that the disease springs from salt, and the absence of vegetable food; it is to their interest to say so. We can cast their flimsy statements to the winds, however, and give them an emphatic contradiction, for their proceedings in this matter will not bear even a partial investigation.

I have gone more fully into this part of my subject than I intended, for the following reason: the advocates of total abstention from salt invariably bring forward scurvy as a conclusive proof70 of their argument, and as unanswerable; they have not looked at it, I am afraid, from the above standpoint, and I think if they will take the trouble to go into the matter more thoroughly, they will find that scurvy originates, not from wholesome salted provisions and the want of vegetables, but from impure and putrid food, which too many owners of ships, from pecuniary motives, prefer to supply, not for the passengers—that would of course be unwise policy—but for the men who labour for them on the waters, and who are at the mercy of employers as insatiable and inexorable in obtaining their pounds of flesh as the storm-tossed ocean yawning for its victims.

"Digestion is the process by which those parts of our food which may be employed in the formation and repair of the tissues, or in the production of heat, are made fit to be absorbed and added to the blood."

I do not think it will be out of place to make a few cursory observations on the process of digestion, for as scurvy is the result of the ingestion of unwholesome food, we cannot do better than consider the process in relation to salt, and its action on animal and vegetable food while it is in the stomach.

When this organ is empty it is completely inactive; there is no secretion of the gastric juice, and the mucus, which is slightly alkaline or neutral, covers the surface; but immediately food is introduced, the mucous membrane, which was pale, at once becomes turgid, owing to the greater influx of blood; because when any organ has work to perform, it requires an increased supply.

The amount of the gastric juice secreted has been variously estimated to be from ten to twenty pints a day in a healthy adult, and by the following table, we find that salt, or rather the chloride of sodium, is present in a considerable quantity. Looking, then, at the immense secretion of the gastric juice, salt is really in continual requisition, making it self-evident that if the supply is not kept up in the same ratio, digestion is retarded, the food passes out of the stomach in an undigested state into the duodenum, and the stomach is consequently overstrained because of the loss of one of its most important constituents; the supply of salt not being equal to the demand.

Composition of Gastric Juice.

Water	994·40
Solid Constituents	5·59
	———
Ferment, Pepsine (with a trace of Ammonia)	3·19
71Hydrochloric Acid	0·20
Chloride of Calcium	0·06
Chloride of Sodium	1·46
Chloride of Potassium	0·55
Phosphate of Lime, Magnesia, and Iron	0·12

In a sheep's gastric juice there is to 971·17 of water, 4·36 of chloride of sodium, showing at once how highly necessary it is for cattle to be supplied with it; a sheep will consume on the average half an ounce of salt daily; that it tends to prevent an outbreak of the rot, I have already drawn the attention of the reader.54

There is we see 0.20 of *hydrochloric acid* to 994.40 of water in the gastric juice, though some are of an opinion that it is *lactic acid*; the weight of evidence is decidedly in favour of *free* hydrochloric acid.

Food when it is going through the process of digestion is reduced to a pulp by the solvent properties of the gastric juice, which are due to the presence of the animal matter or pepsine, and the hydrochloric acid; neither of these two constituents can digest separately, they must be together; and they must be in that proportion as we have before us in the preceding table; to act as complete disintegrators and solvents.

The general effect of digestion is the conversion of the food into what is called *chyme*; and though the various materials of a meal are entirely dissimilar in their composition, whether they are azotised or nitrogenous, and non-azotised or non-nitrogenous; when they are once reduced to this condition, viz., *chyme*, they hardly admit of recognition.

The reader may naturally suppose "that the readiness with which the gastric fluid acts on the several articles of food, is in some measure determined by the state of division, and the tenderness and moisture of the substance presented to it," and he may also be aware of the fact, that the readiness with which any substance is acted upon by the gastric juice, does not necessarily imply that it possesses nutritive characteristics, for it stands to reason that a substance may be nutritious, and yet hard to digest; and when this is the case, the gastric follicles supply a greater quantity of fluid, in order to effect the conversion of the food into chyme. 72 Pepsine and the hydrochloric acid, the two indispensable and inseparable solvents, are consequently secreted in greater abundance in order to meet and overcome the difficulty, so that the food may be in a condition fit for assimilation with the various tissues.

Man requires a mixed kind of aliment, therefore he must have animal as well as vegetable food, though there are many instances of people who live wholly on animal or vegetable substances; these of course are anomalies, and therefore their habits are unnatural. Vegetarianism is a foolish freak of the weak-minded and semi-ignorant; the structure of the teeth of man points conclusively to the fact that he is both carnivorous and herbivorous; though these vegetable philosophers would have us believe that he is destined to feed upon cabbages!

Food is divided into two groups, nitrogenous and non-nitrogenous, or animal and vegetable; the only non-nitrogenous organic substances of the animal, or nitrogenous, are furnished by the fat, and in some few cases by those vegetable matters that may happen to be in the organs of digestion of those animals who are eaten whole.

Nutritive or plastic, is given to those principles of food which are converted into fibrine or albumen of blood, and being assimilated by the various tissues through its medium, and those principles comprising the major part of the non-nitrogenous food, in the form of fat, gum, starch, and sugar, and other substances of a similar nature, are supposed to be utilised in the production of heat, and are termed calorifaciant, or sometimes respiratory food. The principal ordinary articles of vegetable food contain identical substances, in composition, with the fibrine, caseine, and albumen, which constitute the chief nutritive materials of animal food; for instance, the gluten which is present in corn is identical in composition with fibrine, and is therefore called vegetable fibrine; legumen, which exists in beans, peas, and other seeds of the leguminosæ, is similar to the caseine of milk; and albumen is most abundant in the seeds and juices of nearly all vegetables.

On carefully analysing the preceding remarks on food and some of its uses after it has been digested, and the composition and properties of the gastric juice, it is obvious that salt is not only a simple adjunct to food, and therefore not of much importance, but is an article of diet in every sense of the word, and as necessary, if not more so, than many aliments which are regarded as essential.

73

In its relations to animal or nitrogenous, and vegetable or non-nitrogenous, food, salt is in every respect important.

The hydrochloric acid of the gastric juice, which is so bountifully secreted by the glands of the stomach, of course drains the whole system of its salt, and especially does it draw the chloride of sodium from the blood, which contains $3 \cdot 6$ in 1000, being held in solution by the liquor-sanguinis.

Animal or nitrogenous food contains only a minimum of salt, which chiefly exists in the muscular tissue, its principal constituents being albumen and fibrine; if, therefore, it is eaten as a rule without salt, digestion is by no means facilitated, because meat being comparatively tough, the glands have to secrete an increased quantity in order to break down or disintegrate it, and there is, as I have observed, a greater drain on the system.

Vegetable or non-nitrogenous food contains potash; only those vegetables growing near the sea contain soda. The same reasons which apply to animal food hold good as regards vegetable, with this difference: the gluten, the legumen, and their other ingredients are acted upon by the gastric juice more rapidly, and that being the case, a less amount is required, and as a natural consequence less salt, or rather chloride of sodium, is abstracted from the blood; because the more the stomach is called upon to exert itself, a greater flow of blood to that viscus is the result, which takes place only when the food to be acted upon is of a harder or tougher material than ordinary, when the organ is filled to repletion, or when salt is omitted as a rule.

Another fact should be borne in mind: cellulose is a substance invariably present in the vegetable kingdom, and is found both in low and high plants; it is present in the fungus as well as in the palm, in the lichen as well as in the oak; it is not subject to climatic influences nor to atmospheric changes, so that its quantity in all plants is always the same. This cellulose is almost identical in its composition with starch, which is a substance entirely non-nutritious. When in the system starch undergoes a transformation, by some process not as yet clearly defined, into sugar; whether in the stomach or by some action of the liver, physiologists are uncertain, but it is an unexplained physiological fact, nevertheless. Sugar, we know, is a very active agent in the production of fat; therefore it is not desirable for us to have an overplus, but rather to keep it under. Salt is not a fat-producer; it has an opposite74 effect; therefore it should be used plentifully with vegetable food in order to neutralise the effect of the starch or cellulose.

We thus see that this substance cellulose is identical with starch; that starch is turned into sugar, and that sugar promotes the growth of fat. I have already mentioned that stout and fat persons require more salt than those who are spare; therefore we may see at a glance how necessary it is for us to use salt liberally with oleaginous food, and indeed with all which tends to increase the adipose tissue.

Those who have a predisposition to obesity, and who wish to reduce their bulk, cannot take better means to obtain the object of their desire than to use salt at all their meals, and to take care that their food is of the plainest; then with a proper amount of exercise and attention to the secretions, they will find that instead of carrying a distended, cumbersome abdomen about with them, attended with miserable inconveniences, they will have the felicity of experiencing not only a diminution of size, but a more easy and expeditious locomotion; and they will be enabled to

"Cleanse the stuff'd bosom of that perilous stuff

Which weighs upon the heart."

If they wish to effect their purpose more speedily, Glauber's salt waters, which contain salt, can be taken with advantage, for they decrease the fat and assist digestion and assimilation. "In the same way chloride of sodium may be shown to be a more important ingredient than is sometimes supposed. It stimulates gently the mucous membrane of the alimentary canal, and also the muscular fibres of the intestines; when absorbed it promotes tissue-change, and apparently aids the cell formation. Its digestive action is well known."55

According to Dr. Rawitz, who has examined microscopically the products of artificial digestion and the excreta after the same food, cells, both animal and vegetable, pass through the alimentary canal completely unchanged, such as cartilage and fibro-cartilage, except that of fish, which fact is indicative that it is more digestible than any other aliment; elastic fibre is also unchanged, and fat-cells are frequently found altogether unaltered; also after eating fat pork, the pabulum of the lower classes, crystals of cholesterine are invariably to be obtained from the excreta.

Quantities of cell-membrane of vegetables are found in the alvine 75evacuations, likewise starch-cells, with only part of their contents removed, and the green colouring principle, chlorophylle, is never changed.

From the foregoing we see at once the kind of food necessary, as regards its sustentative and nutritious properties, and that which merely serves as an unimportant adjunct.

Dr. Rawitz does not inform us whether a greater or lesser amount of salt was used in his experiments; being regarded as an unimportant item, he probably may have been indifferent as to whether it was used or not, and took no note of the quantity. As nothing was found in the excreta belonging to fish, we may regard it as favouring the view, that being impregnated with salt, and living in salt water, the facility with which it is digested is mainly owing to the presence of salt. Fresh-water fish, as is well known, are not digested so easily and thoroughly as those which live in the sea. Again, Dr. Rawitz does not tell us whether the fish used in his experiments were salt or fresh; I conclude that they were salt, because the consumption of fresh-water fish is considerably below the number of that caught at sea.

Those who believe that man is an organism of vegetable proclivities, and would have him live upon vegetables exclusively, who point with a triumphant smile to scurvy as resulting solely from long-continued abstention from vegetable food, combined with the ingestion of salted meat, should remember that any kind of food indulged in to the exclusion of others injures the health, reduces the physical strength, and deteriorates the blood. They are right as far as their argument goes, but they lose sight of some very remarkable facts when they describe scurvy as originating from salt.

Vegetables which are generally used as aliment are young and fresh; on board ship, and especially in long voyages, they are in nine cases out of ten old and musty, and those belonging to the compositæ, such as cabbages, rapidly degenerate into decomposition, generating a very poisonous gas, viz. sulphuretted hydrogen; while those belonging to the leguminosæ, as peas and beans, lose their great nutritive principle, legumen, which is identical with the caseine of milk, and which renders them such invaluable articles of diet. Besides, if vegetables are kept for any length of time, even if excluded from the air, they are liable to rapid decomposition immediately they are exposed to its influences. I therefore think, as I have asserted already, that salted meat is not wholly respon76sible for scurvy, and that it much more frequently arises from its being salted in the early stages of putrescence.

These vegetable reformers and abstainers from salt are, I am afraid, ignorant of these facts.

If mankind were to act in accordance with the wishes of visionaries, and those who are prone to scientific credulity, and who look upon themselves as philanthropic philosophers, we should speedily be reduced to the unenviable condition of the Frenchman's horse; for to some, animal food is pernicious, salt is in some respects poisonous, water is to be discarded as worse than useless, stimulants in the hour of sickness are to be avoided, and are never to be touched; vegetables are mere woody fibre or starch-cells. They are considerate, however; they have left us fish! This staple of food is not yet ostracised.

Happy is the man who lives according to the dictates of nature, temperately and wholesomely, and who does not run like a thoughtless being into extremes, originating from hare-brained fanatics, and from unpractical utilitarians.

Salt is a preventive of those disfiguring eruptions which frequently affect the young about the face and neck, and which in the majority of cases arise from a defective state of the blood. One need only take a stroll through a crowded thoroughfare to find that this is the fact. These young people, instead of possessing complexions which are indicative of health and purity of blood, carry in their countenances unmistakable marks which cannot escape the eye of an observant and discriminating passer-by. If we were to make inquiries, we should find that they are, with few exceptions, absolute strangers to salt, and that probably they have been brought up from their infancy by their parents never to touch it.

This neglect shows the grossest ignorance on the part of these people, and calls for the most stringent censure; it is almost incredible, to find so many unaccustomed to the use of salt, and who never impress upon their children the need of it, and that the continuance of their health is partly dependent upon a daily use of a substance which is a highly important constituent of the blood.

I have drawn my reader's attention to the facts that the blood of scrofulous persons is deficient in salt, that the amount is variable, and that the deficiency is at once discernible in the objectionable condition of the skin of the face and neck; but here we have people enjoying a fair share of health, who, owing to ignorance77 or indifference, are reducing themselves to a state bordering on disease, and who would otherwise be total strangers to those ailments which only attack the impure, the luxurious and intemperate.

We have seen that salt is necessary in the animal economy, otherwise it would not exist as a constituent of the blood. It is equally necessary for the preservation of health; for in the blood of those people who are suffering from disease, we detect a visible decrease. In some cases of fever the diminution is remarkable; if the febrile symptoms increase in severity, we find that there is a corresponding loss of the chloride of sodium. This simple fact alone shows that it is the imperative duty of those who have at heart the well-being of their fellow-creatures, to impress upon them in emphatic language, that if they wish their blood to be in a pure healthy condition, and to be able to ward off the insidious attacks of disease, they must make it a frequent article of diet.

We are all cognisant that disease will be to the end of time one of the scourges of humanity; and at the present day certain maladies are spreading amongst us with the greatest rapidity, all our efforts to eradicate them having been hitherto altogether futile, and the results far from promising. All our medicines, our improved modes of treatment, and our hygienic schemes, ingenious as they undoubtedly are, reflecting the highest honour on their philanthropic originators, have been, and still are to a considerable extent, abortive, and we are still combating with, and succumbing to, this inveterate enemy of mankind.

We do not diet ourselves as we should; in this respect we are far behind the veriest savage, cannibal though he be: he in his natural state obeys the laws and dictates of nature, which we in our civilised state decidedly do not, notwithstanding the assertions of the dreamy philosophers of the day. He sleeps when nature prompts him, regardless of the sun's heat or midnight dews; he eats when he is hungry, and drinks when he is thirsty; he goes through a certain amount of physical fatigue; his clothing is of the simplest kind; his food on the average is the purest; his drink is that natural fluid which we, owing to our high state of civilisation, so pertinaciously and foolishly discard; he roams at pleasure either on the desert or in the forest; and his impulses, though savage, are never at variance with nature; he is, in fact, as real a child of nature as an average civilised European is the slave of a falsified nature.

78

Those who have travelled in the islands of the Pacific Ocean have informed us that their inhabitants, with but few exceptions, possess the secret of extracting salt from certain substances, which indicates that even they are fully alive to its virtues, and proves to us, who boast of our superiority, that we are deficient of natural acumen, or that it is marred and stultified by those silly customs arising from that curse of civilisation, fashion, which makes slaves of us all, at least of the weak-minded and frivolous.

At the tables of the wealthy it is perfectly absurd to see the small amount of salt which is placed in the smallest receptacles, as if it were the most expensive article; and it is equally ridiculous to see the host and his guests, in the most finical grotesque manner, help themselves to the almost infinitesimal quantities of salt, as if it were a mark of good breeding and delicacy. This is how we pervert nature; our civilisation is a great good, undoubtedly, but at the same time it is frequently at variance with what is good for us. If the blind votaries of fashion think that it is polite to use the gifts of nature in such a way as to render them comparatively useless, let those who wish to enjoy the blessings of health, pure blood, and a wholesome, transparent skin, refrain from those stupid customs of "good society," which are truly indicative of mental weakness and most profound ignorance.

I have known people who accustom themselves to the use of salt baths, and who talk very glibly of the luxury of sea-bathing, who yet are in complete ignorance of the virtues of salt as a condiment and as a preserver of health, and who try to prove that salt so used is obnoxious, and consequently to be avoided. These salt baths are popular, not because they are beneficial, but by reason of their comparative novelty; and accordingly, many who would not think of using salt with their food, plunge headlong into the sea or into a salt-water bath, with all the vigour possible.

Salt baths are presumed by some to be of great value in gout; Droitwitch in particular is famous for them; many who were considered as incurable have alleged that after having used them, they have returned home cured.

The topical application of salt water to weak joints, etc., has only just come to the front; and by many it is regarded as quite a new remedy; and I have heard some very disparaging observations on the medical profession regarding its negligence to, or indifference of, the restorative properties of salt water, alleging that it has been reluctantly forced to advise it, in deference to the popular79 opinion in its favour. It is indeed a fact that until a few years ago, medical men as a rule were utterly unacquainted with salt water as a remedial agent; and the idea no doubt would have been denounced with as much asperity and contumely as the hydropathic treatment is at the present day, and with as much reason. It is a mistake, however, to assume that it is of recent origin, for my father, Mr. Wm. Barnard Boddy, has been in the habit of advising it for over the last sixty years, and with almost uniform success.

Intestinal worms, which so frequently infest the impure, rendering them somewhat offensive to themselves, generate much more rapidly, and take a firmer hold on their victims, even if there is but partial absence of salt in the blood, and particularly if pork is frequently an article of diet. I have known many instances in which they have been expelled, and the intestines thoroughly freed from them, on a more liberal use of salt, for it is certain death to these parasites, helping to root them out, and destroying them, whether they belong to the tape, the round, or the thread variety.

Children, we know, are more liable to have these parasites than adults, with the exception of the tape-worm; particularly is this the case with those of the labouring and agricultural classes, and with children who are fed upon rich dainties. With regard to the agricultural class, it is, I think, easily explained. People who live in the country—I refer, of course to the poorer sort—allow their children to run about wherever they please, especially in the spring and summer time; the cottage door and the small garden are generally the places where they assemble; or the neighbouring lane or meadow, if the weather is at all favourable; where they may be seen rolling and tumbling about, picking up what they can find if at all edible, and soon putting their discoveries into their mouths with apparent relish. The British cottagers, not being at all particular as to whether their vegetables are clean or not, swallow, as well as their children, any insect that may be ensconced in the half-cooked cabbage, or unwashed celery or water-cress. Another reason is, I think, of more weight than the preceding two, and that is, they very seldom think of using salt at meal-time, though it is sometimes to be seen on their tables. The English working-classes are nearly, if not altogether, unacquainted with the benefit of salt, and very few indeed utilise it as they should; so that we can easily understand why80 they are so infested with intestinal parasites, which thrive in such a soil, and increase, in some instances to an enormous extent.

The embryo of the tape-worm, called the *echino-coccus hominis*, in such cases finds a fitting and a secure home, and soon develops into its tape-like form, and with wonderful tenacity keeps firm hold; so that sometimes it is difficult, or even impossible, to effect its entire removal, especially if it has existed for any length of time, and particularly if the individual indulges often in pork; for as its source is undoubtedly measely pork, such a course of diet nourishes it and imparts an increased vitality. I have known them to exist in some people notwithstanding the most energetic and judicious treatment, not only for many years, but for a lifetime; and in the end to cause the death of their victim. Sailors, by reason of their wretched diet, are frequently troubled with this parasite.

Whenever these intestinal parasites exist they are indicative, not only of foul diet and abstention from salt, but also of impure habit, and prove conclusively that the individual is more or less a stranger to salt.

The latter is more commonly the origin of these pests, and shows us how careful we ought to be as to what we eat; for we may well suppose that the ingestion of pork, vegetables half-washed, and abstention from salt is just the kind of diet favourable for the reception of the embryo, and for its speedy development.

Lord Somerville, in his address to the Board of Agriculture some years ago, states that the ancient laws of Holland "ordained men to be kept on bread alone, *unmixed with salt*, as the severest punishment that could be inflicted upon them in their moist climate: the effect was horrible; these wretched criminals are said to have been *devoured by worms*, engendered in their own stomachs."

In the *Medical and Physical Journal* (vol. xxxix.) Mr. Marshall tells us of a lady who had a "natural" (I should say unnatural) aversion to salt, and who was afflicted with worms during the whole of her lifetime. Can we imagine anything more horrible or more disgusting than a person, owing to a foolish prejudice, being in such a foul and impure condition? The enjoyment of life was out of the question, and there can be no doubt that she was in a constant state of ill-health; she must have been, if she had any refined feelings, loathsome to herself, and yet, at the present time, there81 are many in the same plight, who would not touch the smallest particle of salt on any account whatever, or probably would do so with extreme reluctance.

There is another very interesting parasite called the *cysticercus cellulosæ*, originating from diseased pork; it is found in subjects of the leuco-phlegmatic temperament; it is met with in the muscles of the thigh, in the muscular tissue of the heart, and in the brain and eye. If the pork containing this parasite is well soaked in strong brine and thoroughly cooked, no harm will accrue; another fact, I must observe, showing the great importance of salt as an edible.

The thread-worm, technically termed the *ascaris vermicularis*, generally met with in children, is speedily got rid of if a solution of salt is injected into the rectum, combined with the administration of an anthelmintic and pure diet, with a regular use of salt, and a little attention to cleanliness.

While we are upon this question of worms we may with some advantage consider that modern disease—if we may designate parasitical development in muscular tissue as such—which has for some time riveted the attention of scientists, and has all but foiled their endeavours to elucidate; I refer to *trichinosis*, a condition caused by the introduction of a most minute organism, called the *trichina spiralis* (from its being coiled up in transparent capsules), in various muscles of the body, and particularly in the deltoids and other muscles of the arms. Sporadic outbreaks of this incurable disease have occurred at various times and of variable intensity, but always with the most alarming results.

Unfortunately we possess no means of detecting the *trichinæ* when they have once been introduced into the system; we may by the symptoms be led to suspect that they are present, but that is as far as we can go; and if we are to believe Professors Delpech and Reynal it is utterly impossible to discover them; they affirm, however, that in cut meat the larval capsules, or lemon-shaped cases, can only just be seen by the aid of a powerful lens.

In the outbreak which took place in the year 1863 at Heltstaädt, 28 out of 153 persons succumbed; sufficiently exemplifying the fatal character of these infinitesimal organisms; for they may exist in thousands, and even in millions—some say twenty millions—in their miserable victim. So virulent is the disease originating from this parasite, and so insidious in its operation, that in its primary stage it is liable to be mistaken for rheumatism, on account82 of the severe muscular pain; and in fact the sensitiveness of this tissue is so much increased that those muscles which are concerned in the mechanism of respiration give rise to such excruciating pain that the sufferer is quite unable to sleep; indeed, so extreme is the muscular sensibility that the slightest pressure causes acute suffering.

The latter stages simulate typhoid fever, or more correctly, the disease drifts into a typhoid condition, for the symptoms are of that peculiar exceptional character which are presumed to be indicative of this much misunderstood fever. It has, however, been ascertained that those attacked are rarely, if ever, able to endure the long and exhausting course of this disease, but break down, utterly worn out by the unceasing ravages of these prolific and voracious little parasites.

The French, with that acuteness which is natural to them, soon discovered that by good and thorough cooking the *trichinæ* can be destroyed; and they further ascertained that they cannot survive a temperature of 167° Fahrenheit, and also discovered that if meat is *well salted* the *trichinæ* are rendered perfectly harmless; in fact, they are killed by the chloride of sodium quite as effectively as by the application of heat.

This is another unanswerable argument in favour of a more general use of salt, quite sufficient to convince the most stubborn disbeliever; for here we have a parasite which may at any time be introduced into the stomach, let us be as careful as we may; capable of generating myriads in an almost incredible short space of time, and which it is next to impossible to effect the removal of; in the end causing much physical suffering, and producing symptoms liable to be mistaken for those of a dangerous disease; and finally disintegrating those muscles in the fibres of which they live, procreate, and gradually destroy the life of a human being.

The greatest triumph of engineering skill the world has ever seen, the St. Gothard railway tunnel, was the cause of a great sacrifice of life and health owing to a disease engendered by the presence of intestinal parasites, resembling the *trichinæ*; and we learn from Professor Calderini, of Parma, and Professors Bozzolo and Pagliani, of Turin, that from 70 to 80 per cent. of the miners suffered from this complaint, which they have designated *anæmia ankylostoma*. Among the men who worked in the tunnel for about one year 95 per cent. were more or less affected; they likewise83 discovered that those who are thus attacked never entirely recover. Many reasons for this enormous fatality have been assigned, such as the vitiated state of the atmosphere, the difficulty of ventilation, the continual explosions of dynamite, the consumption of which was 660 lb. per day, the smoke and smell from 400 to 500 oil-lamps, and the exhalations from the men and horses. There was an entire absence of sanitary appliances, and the temperature was generally between 80° and 95° Fahrenheit. These surroundings were quite sufficient to account for this great sacrifice of human life, not to mention other causes.

The diet of these men was probably insufficient and of inferior quality, and I dare say if more crucial inquiries were instituted we should find that these miners were as a rule inattentive to personal cleanliness, and that they never used salt at any of their meals; if this were so, and I cannot help thinking that my surmises are correct, we have one great cause all but sufficient for bringing about a condition of the system favourable for the development of *anæmia ankylostoma*.

The presence of these parasites in the intestines of the men who worked in the St. Gothard Tunnel has been proved beyond question by a careful and prolonged series of microscopic examinations by Dr. Giaccone, a physician in the employ of the contractors at Airolo. It is stated that Dr. Sonderreger, of St. Gall, who has been assisting Dr. Giaccone in his experiments, has discovered a process by which these parasites may be completely extirpated.

A pestiferous atmosphere is bad enough in itself, but when it is associated with impure diet—and food I maintain is impure if it is cooked and eaten without salt—we have a state of things which will prepare a soil where intestinal parasites will develop to a marvellous extent.

It is somewhat interesting to know that a similar disease is endemic in Egypt and Brazil, and that it arises from the presence of the *ankylostoma* in the intestines.

Poor diet no doubt is the real cause of this condition, and a great proportion of the inhabitants, as is well known, of these two countries subsist principally on food, not only non-nutritious, but impure in the extreme, which being coupled with the fact of habitual abstention from salt, brings about, as I have said before, a condition of things very favourable for the reception, generation, and development of parasitical organisms.

The outbreak which occurred in the St. Gothard tunnel originated84 from the impurity of the food with which the workmen were supplied, and the absence of salt, could we but fathom the real truth of the matter, though we must not lose sight of the fact that the surroundings were every way calculated to facilitate the growth of disease.

The medicinal properties of mineral waters are of great value in some conditions of the system, especially those resulting from high living and when associated with habitual indulgence in those alcoholic beverages which tend to cause congestion of the liver. These people are not what one would designate as intemperate, but whose partial physical prostration and irregularity of the secretions have been brought about by luxurious living and the unnecessary use of stimulants, combined with unhealthful indolence, and other pernicious habits, which are considered to be of the highest importance by those unhappy votaries of fashion.

Thousands of patients, and many who fancy that they are such, flock to those localities which are famous for their mineral waters; thousands go and thousands return, some better, some worse, and some in the same state of health as when they started: all declare that they are better for their trip, and it may be only a few are acquainted with the constituents of the water they have been drinking; many, if they knew that they are all derived from rock-salt, and that the other constituents to which their curative powers are ascribed are only added as the brine ascends to the surface, would be not a little amazed at their inconsistencies: to refuse to eat salt at meal-time because it is supposed to be deleterious, and then to drink, it may be, tumblerfuls of the solution, is somewhat curious.

As all mineral waters originate from rock-salt, and as they all owe their other constituents to superincumbent strata, it would not be unreasonable to suggest that the chloride of sodium is, *prima facie*, their principal ingredient, and that their beneficial effects are to a certain extent due to it, more than to the presence of those from which their names are derived; though of course there is no denying the fact that some mineral waters are more suitable for some constitutions than others.

One would not advise individuals of plethoric habits to drink those waters which are termed chalybeate, nor those whose kidneys are affected to drink acidulous or carbonated waters; we should recommend quite the reverse.

Mineral waters have a somewhat evanescent popularity; one is85 rapidly succeeded by another: one that was highly eulogised is now neglected, and those which are now in favour will be, in all probability, discarded in a few years. At the present time there are many, though not a few holding a very precarious position in public estimation.

Glauber's Salt Waters, as the name indicates, owe their medicinal properties to the presence of the sulphate of soda, chloride of sodium, and other salts. They are more nauseous than Epsom salts, and slightly more irritating; the first may depend upon the condition of the palate, the other on the weakness or obstinacy of the alimentary canal. These waters contain saline aperients which exercise no little influence on the change of tissue; a result which should make them find great favour with patients who wish to diminish their bulk without affecting their muscles.

These waters contain the chloride of sodium, the presence of which is, in my opinion, of more benefit than all the other salts put together, and which, if absent, would deprive the waters of their efficacy, or at least effect such modifications as would render them practically of but little use.

All these mineral waters come from brine-springs, and whether they are called chalybeate, carbonated, saline, or hepatic waters, whether they come from Spa or Tunbridge Wells, from Carlsbad or Ilkestone, from Püllna or Cheltenham, Buxton, Friedrichshall, Droitwich, or Wiesbaden, their common origin is rock-salt, and to that mineral alone their virtues are principally due; the iron, magnesia, lime, and the other salts which they collect on their upward course are merely accessories, and are more useful to the proprietors than to the credulous recipients. They are purged freely, they are dieted carefully, and the blood is purified, and the result is of course beneficial; they could do the same at home, but then a weak solution of salt and magnesia or iron looks very homely when put side by side with some Carlsbad56 or Friedrichshall waters: there is a great deal in a name, and the more nauseous a compound is the greater are its medicinal virtues; so think some.

86

In all fevers, whether epidemic, endemic, or sporadic, the blood is thicker than ordinary, by reason of an increase of the fibrine and a decrease of the chloride of sodium; because the fibrine, which always has a tendency to coagulate, is not kept in check by the solvent properties of the chloride of sodium; this alone accounts for their partiality for salt.

In rheumatic fever the blood is even thicker than it is in other fevers; in acute rheumatism the patient is generally bathed in profuse perspiration night and day, and the sweat contains a good deal of lactic acid. The acid in the gastric juice is supposed by some physiologists to be lactic acid, whilst others affirm that it is hydrochloric acid; there is, however, such a similitude that one acid is barely distinguishable from the other. The blood in this fever therefore loses much more salt than in other febrile conditions, which explains the acute pain in the joints and the desire the patient has for salt. Blood in a thickened condition cannot pass through the blood vessels near joints without giving much pain, owing to the unyielding nature of the parts; and the fibrine also has a tendency to stagnate if the blood does not flow as it should.

In some cases of sickness, when not accompanied with vomiting, half a teaspoonful of salt in a little water is sometimes most effective. Whenever there is a feeling of nausea the stomach is relaxed, there is the usual amount of the gastric juice, but it is deficient of the hydrochloric acid; therefore a small solution of salt takes the place really of the acid, and the sickness is relieved, it likewise supplies the chloride of sodium, which has been abstracted from the gastric fluid.

In violent attacks of colic, if there is no other remedy at hand, a teaspoonful of salt in a pint of cold water, which the patient may sip, is most speedy in relieving the sufferer. The same will also relieve a person who has had a heavy fall and is partly unconscious.

In hæmorrhage from the lungs, when the usual remedies have failed, a solution of salt will sometimes arrest it. When applied to a cut the bleeding ceases. These little facts are well worth knowing, because salt is always to be found in every home, and so may be given or applied in case there is no medical man at hand; matrons and nurses of small hospitals, infirmaries, and workhouses should be acquainted with them in case of an emergency.

We have now before us the properties of salt in a medical and87 dietetic sense; that indirectly it is a therapeutical agent of some value cannot be denied; that it is an important aliment is a fact which cannot be explained away; and that it is a preserver of health all must allow.

That it is of a deleterious tendency is a mere assertion as unsubstantial as "thin air," and as flimsy as gossamer—*magno conatu, magnas nugas.*

CHAPTER VIII.

PHYSIOLOGICAL PROPERTIES.

Prejudice is the daughter of ignorance; and nothing exemplifies the truth of this more thoroughly than the senseless repugnance to salt which is now so remarkably prevalent. Ask these persons for their reasons, if we can dignify them as such, for disliking salt; their answers, as a rule, will be trifling platitudes, altogether unworthy of refutation, or even of moderate attention.

Objections founded on imperfect, or an affectation of knowledge, are not worth the trouble of confuting, even if they be supported by a fair amount of intelligence; but when the opponents of salt begin to base their assertions upon science, and demur on medicinal, dietetic, and physiological grounds, then we must meet them armed with similar weapons to those they have chosen, with the handling of which they are but imperfectly acquainted, and which therefore recoil upon them in such a way as prove that though they may be shrewd, they are but badly informed and credulous scientists.

At the present day the science of physiology has arrived at such a pitch of perfection that there is not a single secretion, tissue, or organ of the body, with the exception of the spleen, which has not been investigated, and the functions divulged and made so plain that it is quite divested of that apparent mystery which formerly enshrouded it; though our kind friends, the anti-vivisectionists, would willingly adopt the most unjust measures to prevent the study of life from being more perfect than it already is: they protest with well-feigned horror at a frog or a rabbit, under the influence of chloroform, being experimented upon for the benefit of humanity, while they see, without allowing a sign of disapprobation to escape from them, an inoffensive hare chased to death for88 the amusement of gentility, and probably gloat over, with pleasure, the dying agonies of a stag: a sight which gratifies the somewhat questionable proclivities of refined and elegant ladies, who race their horses out of breath to gaze on the sanguinary scene.

Had it not been for physiological research we should not have known that the chloride of sodium was such an important constituent in the animal economy; we should have been in utter ignorance of the science of life, and we should never have known how man is begotten, how developed, or how he dies. With regard to the two processes of decay and repair, or how the human organism, from a mere cell, gradually becomes a being highly organised, mentally as well as physically, we should have known nothing. Physiology has been a boon to humanity and an inexhaustible field of research to the scientific.

In a chemical point of view there is no more important mineral constituent in the human body than the chloride of sodium, for it occurs nearly in every part of the system, both solid and fluid, in close and intimate relation with the organic compounds, and it materially influences their chemical and physical properties; for instance, the albumen partly owes its solubility to the presence of salt, the quantity of which causes the differences which it presents as regards its coagulation; pure caseine, which is quite insoluble, is dissolved at once on the addition of common salt; and if it is added in increased proportions it impedes the coagulation of the fibrine. Another remarkable physiological fact is that the chloride of sodium is not only uniformly present, but its various proportions are nearly definite and constant, both in the fluids and tissues;

and the existence of a provision for the limitation of the quantity kept in the system causes the proportions to be little affected, in the way of excess at least, by the amount of salt the food may contain, that is, if the diet is wholesome and the individual healthy.

According to Lehmann, who experimentalised on himself, the blood may contain in a normal state 4·14 parts of the chloride of sodium in 1000, and after a meal of very salty food it may be only increased to 4·15; he says it only rose to 4·18 when two ounces of salt had been taken an hour before, and two quarts of water had been drunk in the interval. The blood will not receive more than a certain amount; and as an over-amount of salt will produce extreme thirst, a quantity passes through the kidneys with the water that has been drunk; frequent drinking of course causes frequent micturition. If we take the mean of numerous observations by several89 experimenters, the average quantity of urine voided by healthy adult males is about 52-1/2 fluid ounces; this quantity may contain urea to the amount of 512·4 grains, chlorine 105·0 grains, and soda 125·? grains, besides other salts and extractives. If such an amount passes out with the urine we can easily account for the slight increase in the blood of Lehmann.

The quantity of the chloride of sodium in the blood is liable to great variation in different diseases; and there can be little doubt that this variation is closely connected (though whether in the relation of cause or in that of effect, we are not exactly entitled to surmise) with the histological and other transformations of the component parts of the blood. The proportions of salt greatly differ in several tissues, and also at different periods of the development of the same tissue. "Thus in muscle," according to Enderlin, "100 parts of the ash left after incineration of ox-flesh yielded nearly 46 per cent. of the chloride of sodium and potassium; which, as this ash constitutes 4·23 per cent. of the dried flesh, would give 1·94 as the proportion of the chloride of sodium in 100 parts of the latter; and reckoning this dried residue to constitute 28 per cent. of the whole substance of the muscle (the remaining 77 parts being water) the proportion of chloride of sodium in the latter will be 0·44. These figures, as will be presently seen, bear a remarkably close correspondence to those which represent the proportion of chloride of sodium in the ash, solid residue and entire mass of the blood."57

Next to muscle, cartilage contains the largest amount of the chloride of sodium, and this especially in the temporary cartilages of the fœtus, its place being taken by the phosphate of lime as it approaches the time of birth. The percentage of the chloride of sodium contained in the ash of the costal cartilage of an adult is about 8·2; in the laryngeal cartilage 11·2; but as the ash does not constitute above 3·4 per cent. of the entire substance the percentage of the chloride of sodium in the latter is, at the most, 0·38 of the whole, or less than that of blood and muscle. Only from 0·7 to 1·5 per cent. could be extracted from the ash of bone.

Besides the important uses of the chloride of sodium in the blood to which we have already adverted, it serves the purpose of furnishing the hydrochloric acid required (by many animals, at least) for the gastric secretion; and it likewise supplies the soda-base for the alkaline phosphate, whose presence in the blood appears90 to serve a most important purpose in the respiratory process. Moreover, there is reason to think, from the experiments of Boussingault upon animals, as well as from other considerations, that the presence of salt in the blood and excreted fluids facilitates the deportation of excrementitious substances from the blood. The proportion in which it occurs in the principal animal fluids is represented by the following table, constructed by

Lehmann chiefly from his own analyses; it is highly interesting, and shows us at a glance that it is more important in the economy than any other substance, and is significant of the fact that health cannot exist long if the chloride of sodium is below the normal amount.

Percentage of Chloride of Sodium in various Animal Fluids, their Solid Residue and their Ash.

	Liquid.	Solid Residue.	Ash.
Human Blood	0·421	1·931	57·641
Blood of Horse	0·510	2·750	67·105
Chyle	0·531	8·313	67·884
Lymph (Nasse)	0·412	8·246	72·902
Serum of Blood (Nasse)	0·405	5·200	59·090
Blood of the Cat (Nasse)	0·537	2·826	67·128
Chyle (Nasse)	0·710	7·529	62·286
Human Milk	0·087	0·726	33·089
Saliva	0·153	12·988	62·195
Gastric Juice of Dog	0·126	12·753	42·089
Human Bile	0·364	3·353	30·464
Mucus (Nasse)	0·583	13·100	70·000
Serum of Pus (Nasse)	1·260	11·454	72·330

We have thus proved physiologically that the chloride of sodium holds a most prominent position among the other constituents of the body; that it is present in considerable quantities in muscle as well as in the blood; and that it furnishes the acid, which is necessary for the stomach to perform its functions of digestion. It holds the albumen partly in solution, and its coagulation is dependent more or less on the amount of salt which is present in the blood, and it also possesses the power of preventing the coagulation of the fibrine. In fevers the blood is generally thicker, and has a tendency to coagulate by reason of the partial absence of salt, because a good deal passes off with the perspiration; and fever patients always prefer salt to sugar, for while one refreshes them and helps to restore the usual healthy tone of the palate, by constringing the papillæ of the tongue, the other raises feelings of disgust.

It is also present in cartilage, though in a lesser degree than in blood or muscle, because in cartilage there is no disintegration or91 waste of tissue, and therefore it does not require such a perpetual supply; there is, on the contrary, a continual loss going on in muscle, especially during exertion. Perspiration is to a certain extent the principal medium which carries off the chloride of sodium, owing to its being held in solution by the liquor-sanguinis; during fatigue, particularly if prolonged, a greater quantity passes off, producing various degrees of thirst. That the normal proportion of the chloride of sodium should be regularly maintained must be obvious.

In febrile disease the fibrine of the blood is materially increased, and there is also a marked decrease of salt, which is dependent on a greater or lesser intensity of the attack, rendering the blood denser, owing to the fact of the tendency of the fibrine to coagulate by reason of the diminution of the chloride of sodium, causing the blood to circulate slowly and with difficulty.

In some other morbid conditions, which we have already noticed, the blood becomes thinner and poorer; and consequently the system degenerates, and we get an anæmic, or chlorotic tendency, especially if there is a scrofulous diathesis. There are other blood diseases, as the reader may suppose, and which are more truly such, than those to which I have just alluded, into the phenomena of which it is not necessary to enter.

In health what a decided difference! the specific gravity of the blood is uniformly equable;58 it circulates with comparative ease; and the whole system is permeated with the life-giving and health-preserving chloride of sodium, and the coagulation of the fibrine is prevented by nothing else but that mineral and inorganic substance—salt, which at the same time purifies and maintains the equalisation of the constituents of the blood. By it also the hydrochloric acid is supplied to the stomach, enabling that organ to perform its functions of digestion in accordance with the laws of health; and it likewise furnishes the alkaline phosphate "whose presence in the blood appears to serve the most important purpose in the respiratory process."

What stronger evidence do we require to prove the salutary efficacy of salt? No wonder that it is so frequently reverted to in Holy Writ; neither can it be a source of surprise that it has been so carefully cherished and extensively utilised from time immemorial. What is to be regarded as an extraordinary anomaly is that there are not a few who are entire strangers to its virtues, 92and who prefer impurity and defilement to the luxury of health and cleanliness.

Those who desire more conclusive proof of the utility of salt, of its necessity in the animal economy, and of the peculiar morbid phenomena to which its absence in the system gives rise, I would refer to two articles which appeared at different times in the *Medical Press and Circular*, and in the *Medical Times and Gazette*.59 The cases I there mention occurred in different localities, and they demonstrate incontestably that parasites, especially the *lumbrici* (the *tæniæ* are well known to infest adults of impure habit), are sometimes the origin of strange and incomprehensible symptoms of a deceptive character, rendering diagnosis extremely difficult and unsatisfactory, and frequently endangering the lives of the sufferers. Is it not a blessing to know that nature has munificently provided a means whereby these distressing evils may be checked and definitely eradicated by a daily use of such an enemy to, and destroyer of, disease as the chloride of sodium, universally known as common salt?

CHAPTER IX.

CONCLUSION.

It is invariably a relief when one's task is completed, and more so when it is self-imposed. Putting our thoughts and opinions upon paper for others to peruse and to criticise, is pleasure combined with not a little anxiety; for one cannot with any degree of certainty predict what kind of reception one's efforts may have from the public, who are frequently led to a choice of books on the recommendation of critics and reviewers; so that an unknown author is placed at a great disadvantage, and at the mercy of those who may laud a book to the skies if they please, satirically criticise another, and pass over a third with a sarcastic smile or a significant shrug of the shoulders. I am afraid that my little volume will unfortunately be found amongst the latter, but I candidly acknowledge that I hope it will be regarded as belonging to the first, or at least to the second.

93

As I have simply written it in order to point out the virtues of an aliment of the greatest interest in whatever light we may look at it, I trust that if I have not instructed, I have at any rate afforded pleasure to those who have thought it worth their while to glance over its pages; and I shall be quite contented if they have derived as much satisfaction in reading, as I have experienced in writing it.

I have tried to impress upon the reader the advisability, and indeed the necessity, of using the bountiful gifts of nature in a manner consistent with common sense, and not to follow blindly and credulously the whims and conceits of others, but to regard their frantic efforts to indoctrinate the thoughtless, with that dispassionate indifference which is the sign of philosophical complacency and superiority. Lucretius says truly that "nothing is more delightful than to occupy the elevated temples of the wise, well fortified by tranquil learning, whence you may look down upon others and see them straying in every direction, and wandering in search of the path of life."

Approbation is pleasing, and particularly so when it comes from those who are more able to judge impartially and correctly than others; and censure, if deserved, though far from gratifying, is not of a nature to intimidate or to create discouragement.

With these concluding remarks, and certain misgivings, I now submit my short work to the indulgent consideration of those who read for the sake of obtaining information, those who read for amusement only, and to those who peruse literary productions with the eye of criticism. Lord Bacon advises us to "Read, not to contradict and confute, nor to believe and take for granted, nor to find talk and discourse, but to weigh and consider. Some books are to be tasted, others to be swallowed, and some few to be chewed and digested. That is, some books are to be read only in parts; others to be read, but not curiously; and some few to be read wholly, and with diligence and attention."

In conclusion, I must say that I sincerely hope that the candid reader has reaped improvement where the critic may have found only matter for censure.

94

APPENDIX.

A., page 38. "Occasionally lakes are found which have streams flowing *into* them, but none flowing *out*. Such lakes are usually salt. The Caspian Sea in Asia is an example. It is called a sea from its great extent, but it is in reality an inland lake of salt water."

B., page 80. Mr. William Barnard Boddy on "Diet and Cholera": "The nourishment we derive from the flesh of some animals is not so compatible with the well-being of our constitutional wants as others, particularly the swine, which was altogether prohibited by the Jewish lawgiver, independent of its spiritual enactments, because it produced 'leprosy.' Now pork is largely consumed in England, especially by the poorer classes, and in ninety-nine cases out of every hundred is almost invariably succeeded by diarrhœa; and we need not be surprised at this when we look at the filthy habits of this animal; its impure feeding and liability to the diseases of measles and scarlet-fever. But when we know that they are often in this state killed and sold as an article of food, the liability to disease of course is much greater. But this is not all, as relates to this class of society, for almost—I might say positively so—every article upon which they subsist is impoverished by vile adulterations, and worse, putrefactions; their limited means enabling them to procure only the half-decomposed refuse of the vegetable market, and the half-tainted meat from the butchers' shambles.

"The more wealthy command all the luxuries of life in abundance, and, agreeable to their inclinations and appetites, feast accordingly. Over-indulgence however, often repeated, at last exhausts the healthy tone of the stomach, and blunts the keen edge of desire; and in order to produce a false appetite, condiments of various95 kinds and degrees are substituted; so that, in fact, the food becomes nearly as vitiated by these additions as that of the poor man's by subtractions—the one of necessity, the other of choice. Extremes meet, and here 'the rich and poor meet together;' for under both circumstances the animal economy must severely suffer, and the 'blood, which is the life,' becomes weak and serous; and though for a time, from the great reluctance health has to depart, the growing evils of an impure and unwholesome diet may not be perceived or apprehended, yet insensibly, from the perpetual inroads made upon the constitution, and the delicate seat of life, the efforts to resist disease become weaker and weaker, till at last the whole mass is left without any internal active principle of sound health available to resist or overcome its effects."

THE END.

BAILLIÈRE, TINDALL & COX, 20, KING WILLIAM STREET, STRAND.

FOOTNOTES:

[1] The saliva, besides containing water, ptyaline, fatty matter, and albumen, holds in solution chloride of sodium and potassium, besides the sulphate of soda and the phosphates of lime and magnesia. The amount secreted during twenty-four hours has been estimated at from two to three pints.

[2] Their food, according to geologists, consisted solely of shell-fish.

[3] This sea is called by several names, viz., "The Dead Sea," "The Sea of the Plain," or "of the Arabah," and "The East Sea." In the 2nd Book of Esdras v. 7, it is called the "Sodomish Sea." Josephus uses a similar name, ἡ Σοδομύτυς λίμνη—the Sodomite Lake; he also calls it by the same name as Diodorus Siculus, the "Asphaltic Lake"—ἡ Ἀσφαλτίτις λίμνη. It contains 26 per cent. of salt, including large quantities of magnesium compounds; its weight is of course great, a gallon weighing almost 12-1/2 lb.; and its buoyancy is proportionate to the weight, being such that the human body cannot sink in it. At the south side is a mass of crystallised salt, and in it is a very peculiar cavern, extending at least five miles, varying in height from 200 to 400 feet. This sea is 1312 feet below the level of the Mediterranean; the river Jordan, from the Sea of Galilee, flows into it, but no river flows from it.

[4] According to C. Velleius Paterculus of Rome, Homer flourished B.C. 968; according to Herodotus, B.C. 884; the Arundelian Marbles fix his era B.C. 907.

[5] To show how acute the Greek mind must have been, and how alive the philosophers of that classic country were to everything, whether beautiful or useful, we need only call to mind the quaint observation of Zeno, the founder of the Stoics, who was born about B.C. 300, and who says that "a soul was given to the hog instead of salt, to prevent his body from rotting;" by this we see he was quite cognisant of the preservative properties of salt.

[6] Between the Nile and the Red Sea there are quarries of white marble, of porphyry, of basalt, and the beautiful green breccia, known as *Verde d'Egitto*; in the same locality are found gold, iron, lead, emerald, and copper.

[7] A learned author states as follows: "We have seen, too, that the earliest state of Egypt, as seen in the pyramids, and in the tombs of the same age, reveals an orderly society and civilisation, of which the origin is unknown."

[8] No doubt they were proud of their African parentage, and looked upon the hoary monarchy of the Nile with a sentiment of religious awe and unfeigned wonder. Baron Bünsen graphically puts it: "Egypt was to the Greeks a sphinx with an intellectual human countenance."

[9] Probably owing to the existence of salt in Western Thibet and in Lahore, a province of Hindostan, also the Indian Salt Range, which stretches in a sigmoid curve, according to the late researches of Mr. Wynne, from Kalabagh on the Indus to a point north of Tank, both the Chinese and Hindoos may have been equally cognisant of its virtues with the Egyptians, especially when

we have it recorded that the Celestials procured it by a process not only original but in a certain degree characteristic of Asiatic combination of ingenuity and clumsiness.

[10] Baron Bünsen says that "No nation of the earth has shown so much zeal and ingenuity, so much method and regularity in recording the details of private life, as the Egyptians." They were also most expert engineers; the canal from the Nile to the Red Sea, which may be called the canal of Rameses II., being protected at the Suez mouth by a system of hydraulic appliances to obviate difficulties arising from the variable levels of the water.

[11] "It is a strange fact that the early Egyptians, like the Hindoos, had a religious dread of the sea,"(?); and yet in the reign of Necho, the son of Psammetichus, they actually accomplished the circumnavigation of Africa: the voyage took three years.

[12] Dr. Draper's "History of the Intellectual Development of Europe."

[13] "One momentous consequence of the Shepherd conquest appears to have been that the expelled Shemites carried back with them into Syria the arts and letters of Egypt, which were thence diffused by the maritime Phœnicians over the opposite shores of Greece. Thus Egypt began at this epoch to come in contact at once with the East and the West, with Asia and with Europe."

[14] "Euterpe," book ii. chap. lxxvii.

[15] Lord Bacon mentions somewhere in his works that the ancients discovered that salt water will dissolve salt put into it in less time than fresh water. The same great philosopher also affirms that "salt water passing through earth through ten vessels, one within another, hath not lost its saltness; but drained through twenty, becomes fresh."

[16] The Russians have a custom of presenting bread and salt to the newly-married bride and bridegroom. In archæology we have salt-silver, one penny at the feast of St. Martin, given by the tenants of some manors, as a commutation for the service of carrying their lord's salt from market to his larder; an old English custom.

[17] According to the researches of the late Mr. George Smith, Babylonian literature is of a much more ancient date than the histories of the Bible; which fact would tend to indicate that the intellectual development of that Eastern monarchy may have been coëval with that of the African.

[18] Dr. Draper's "History of the Intellectual Development of Europe."

[19] Leviticus ii. 13.

[20] 2 Kings ii. 21.

[21] Judges ix. 45.

[22] 2 Chronicles xiii. 5.

[23] Numbers xviii. 19.

[24] Ezekiel xvi. 4.

[25] Job v. 6.

[26] St. Mark ix. 50.

[27] *Ibid.*

[28] Huxley's "Physiography."

[29] Sir Robert Christison's "Treatise on Poisons."

[30] Sea-water contains 2·5 per cent. of the chloride of sodium; some say 4 per cent.; according to others, 5·7.

[31] It is well worth remembering that the Thames carries away from its basin above Kingston 548,230 tons of saline matter annually.

[32] Hence arose the custom of asking for salt at the Eton Montem.

[33] Sir R. S. Murchison, "The Mineral Springs of Gloucestershire and Worcestershire."

[34] Dr. Mantell's "Wonders of Geology."

[35] There are the noted salt-works near Portobello, Edinburgh, which have been so truthfully presented to us on canvas by Mr. Edward Duncan.

[36] In Prussia salt is obtained from the brine-springs of that part of Saxony which is subject to her jurisdiction. It also exists in abundance in Bavaria and Würtemberg; and it is the chief mineral production of the Grand Duchy of Baden.

[37] "In one village they only found one earthen pot containing food, which Bruce took possession of, leaving in its place a wedge of salt, which, strange to say, is still used as small money in Gondar and all over Abyssinia."—Bruce's "Travels in Abyssinia."

[38] Polymnia, book vii. chap. xxx.

[39] The geographical features of this almost unknown country are peculiarly interesting, and are unique when compared with others; the great height of its mountains, its remarkable elevation, the large rivers which take their rise here, and the numerous salt lakes, the altitude of some being from 13,800 to 15,400 feet above the level of the sea, all combine to excite our curiosity, which is increased by the fact that we know next to nothing of the interior or of the habits of the people.

[40] "Many springs in Sicily contain muriate of soda; and the 'fuime salso' in particular is impregnated with so large a quantity that cattle refuse to drink it. There is a hot spring at St. Nectaire, in Auvergne, which may be mentioned as one of many, containing a large proportion of muriate of soda, together with magnesia and other ingredients."—Sir Charles Lyell's "Principles of Geology."

[41] The Jurassic formation presents a remarkable contrast with that of the Triassic, in the profusion of organic remains; for while the latter contains next to none, the former teems with marine fossils, a proof that the strata were unfavourable for the preservation of organic structures.—Dr. Mantell's "Wonders of Geology."

[42] There is a mountain composed entirely of rock-salt not far from this old Moorish city; it is 500 feet in height and three miles in circumference; it is completely isolated, and gypsum is also present. In other countries there are similar enormous masses, which require to be dug out and pulverised by machinery on account of their hardness.

[43] Gypsum, or sulphate of lime, consists of sulphuric acid 46·31, lime 32·90, and water 20·79. The massive gypsum is called *Alabaster*; the transparent gypsum *Selenite*; powdered calcined gypsum forms *Plaster of Paris*. The fibrous gypsum has a silken lustre, and is used for ear-rings, brooches, and other ornaments. Fibrous gypsum of great beauty occurs in Derbyshire; veins and masses of this substance abound in the red marls bordering the valley of the Trent.

[44] *Geological Journal*, vol. iii. p. 257.

[45] Pereira's "Materia Medica," vol. i. p. 581.

[46] Sir Charles Lyell's "Principles of Geology."

[47] In the great desert of Gobi, which is supposed to have been originally the bed of the sea which communicated through the Caspian with the Baltic, as confirmatory of this theory, salt is found in great quantities mixed with the soil. To go a step further, we may infer that the lake in Western Thibet (called Tsomoriri) may have been in prehistoric times joined with this vanished sea, and if so would account for its being saline.

[48] Sir Charles Lyell's "Principles of Geology."

[49] In rocks of igneous origin, of which there are many and varied sorts in Australia, no fossils are found except in those rare cases where animal or vegetable bodies have become invested in a stream of lava or overwhelmed by a volcanic shower.

[50] Pigeons are always attracted by a lump of salt, and there is a kind of bait called a salt-cat which is usually made at salt-works.

[51] "Vestiges of the Natural History of Creation."

[52] See page 28, chap. iii.

[53] During the famine in Armenia in the year 1880 the people were most distressed because they had no means to supply themselves with salt, the want of which they felt even more than the lack of food.

[54] It is an interesting fact that the gastric juice varies in different classes of animals, according to the food on which they subsist; thus in birds of prey as kites, hawks, and owls, it only acts on animal matter, and does not dissolve vegetables; in other birds, and in all animals feeding on grass, as oxen, sheep, and hares, it dissolves vegetable matter, as grass, but will not touch flesh of any kind.

[55] The *Medical Press* "Analytical Reports on the Principal Bottled Waters," by Professor Ticheborne and Dr. Prosser James.

[56] An alkaline spring has just been discovered in Bunhill Row which possesses most of the constituents of Carlsbad water, but in a dilute degree. A tube well, 217 feet in depth, has been recently completed on the premises of Messrs. Le Grand and Sutcliff, artesian well engineers. From an analysis which has been made of the spring found in the chalk it appears to be soft water possessing the characteristics which are peculiar to the above-mentioned famous German Spa. The well, although artesian, is only so to a partial extent, and a pump of a novel construction raises the water from 128 feet, and delivers it at the surface.

[57] Dr. Carpenter's "Human Physiology."

[58] Specific gravity of the blood, 1·055.

[59] "Observations on the Symptoms arising from the Ascaris Lumbricoides," *Medical Press and Circular*, March 13, 1878; "On a Form of Pyrosis caused by the Ascaris Lumbricoides," *Medical Times and Gazette*, June 7, 1879.

3

ALPHABETICAL INDEX OF AUTHORS.

AN
ALPHABETICAL INDEX OF SUBJECTS,

8

9

Africa. A Contribution to the Medical History of our West African Campaigns. By Surgeon-Major Albert A. Gore, M.D., Sanitary Officer on the Staff. Price 10s. 6d.

"Dr. Gore has given us a most interesting record of a series of stirring events in which he took an active part, and of elaborate precautions for the maintenance of health."—*Medical Press.*

Africa. Life on the Gold Coast. Being a full and accurate Description of the Inhabitants, their Modes and Habits of Life; interspersed with amusing Anecdotes, Hints to Travellers and others in Western Africa. By Surgeon-General Gordon, M.D., C.B., Hon. Physician to Her Majesty the Queen. Price 2s. 6d.

Alcohol, in some Clinical Aspects: A Remedy, a Poison. By Godwin Timms, M.D., M.R.C.P. Lond., Senior Physician to the North London Consumption Hospital. Price 1s.

Anæsthetics. The Dangers of Chloroform and the Safety and Efficiency of Ether in Surgical Operations. By John Morgan, M.D., F.R.C.S. Second thousand, price 2s.

Anatomy. Aids to Anatomy. By George Brown, M.R.C.S., Gold Medalist, Charing Cross Hospital, Formerly Demonstrator of Anatomy, Westminster Hospital. Fifth thousand, price 1s. 6d. cloth, 1s. paper wrapper.

"The little book is well done."—*Lancet.*

"With this little work students need have no dread of College Examiners."—*Medical Press.*

Anatomy. Text Book of Anatomical Plates, designed under the direction of Professor Masse, with descriptive Text. By E. Bellamy, F.R.C.S., Surgeon to Charing Cross Hospital, Examiner in Anatomy, Royal College of Surgeons, Professor of Anatomy, Government Science and Art Department. Second edition, price, plain 21s., hand-coloured 42s.

"Undeniably the most beautiful plates we have."—*Lancet.*

"With these plates, the student will be able to read up his anatomy almost as readily as with a recent dissection before him."—*Students' Journal.*

Anatomy. The Essentials of Anatomy. Designed on a new and more easily comprehensible basis, as a Text-book for Students, and as a book of easy reference to the practitioner. By W. Darling, M.D., F.R.C.S. Eng., Professor of Anatomy in the University of New York, and Ambrose L. Ranney, A.M., M.D., Adjunct Professor. Price 12s. 6d.

"The arrangement of the subjects, their detailed treatment, and the methods of memorising, are peculiar to the authors, and are the results of long experience in the teaching of students. There is, in fact, an individuality about the work, which gives it a peculiar value to the student and practitioner."—*New York Medical Record.*

10

Anatomy. The Pocket Gray, or Anatomist's Vade-Mecum. Compiled specially for Students from the works of Gray, Ellis, Holden, and Leonard. Price 2s. 6d.

"A marvellous amount of information has been condensed into a remarkably small space."—*Medical Press.*

Anatomy. Human Anatomy and Physiology, illustrated by a series of Movable Atlases of the Human Body, showing the relative positions of the several parts, by means of Superposed Coloured Plates, from the designs of Prof. G. J. Witkowski, M.D.

⚘ A Companion to every work on Anatomy and Physiology.

Part I.—Neck and Trunk. With Text Descriptive and Explanatory of the physiology and functions of the several parts. By Robert Hunter Semple, M.D., F.R.C.P. Lond. Price 7s. 6d.

Part II.—Throat and Tongue, showing the Mechanism of Voice, Speech, and Taste. Text by Lennox Browne, F.R.C.S. Edin., Senior Surgeon to the Central London Throat and Ear Hospital. Price 7s. 6d.

Part III.—The Female Organs of Generation and Reproduction. Text by James Palfrey, M.D., M.R.C.P. Lond., Senior Obstetric Physician to, and Lecturer on Midwifery and Diseases of Women at, the London Hospital. Price 7s. 6d.

Part IV.—The Eye and the Apparatus of Vision. Text by Henry Power, F.R.C.S., Senior Ophthalmic Surgeon to, and Lecturer on Ophthalmic Surgery at, St. Bartholomew's Hospital, Senior Surgeon to the Royal Westminster Ophthalmic Hospital. Price 7s. 6d.

Part V.—The Ear and Teeth. The Mechanism of Hearing and of Mastication. Text of the Ear by Lennox Browne, F.R.C.S. Edin., Senior Surgeon to the Central London Throat and Ear Hospital; Text of the Teeth by Henry Sewill, M.R.C.S., formerly Dental Surgeon to the West London Hospital. Price 7s. 6d.

Part VI.—The Brain (Cerebrum, Cerebellum, and Medulla Oblongata) and Skull. Text by T. Stretch Dowse, M.D., F.R.C.P. Edin., Physician to the Hospital for Paralysis and Epilepsy, formerly Medical Superintendent of the Central London Sick Asylum. Price 7s. 6d.

Part VII.—The Male Organs of Generation. Text by D. Campbell Black, M.D. Price 7s. 6d.

⁎ No such simple, reliable, and comprehensive method of learning the several parts, positions, and functions of the body has hitherto been attempted; the entire Series being unique, will be most valuable to the Teacher, the Student, and to all who wish to become acquainted with the anatomy and physiology of the human economy.

11

Anatomography; or, Graphic Anatomy. A new method of grasping and committing to memory the most difficult points required of the student. By W. Darling, M.D., F.R.C.S. Eng., Professor of Anatomy in the University of New York. Price 1s.

"We heartily commend the work to the attention of students."—*Students' Journal.*

Artistic Anatomy, for the use of Students in Schools of Art. By John Sparkes, Head Master of the National Art Training Schools, South Kensington. *Shortly*, price 5s.

Artistic Anatomy. Anatomy of the External Forms of Man, designed for the use of Artists, Sculptors, etc. By Dr. J. Fau. Used at the Government School of Art, South Kensington. Twenty-nine plates. Folio; price, plain 24s., coloured 42s.

Artistic Anatomy. Elementary Artistic Anatomy of the Human Body. From the French of Dr. Fau. Text, translated by Dr. Carter Blake, Lecturer on Anatomy at the Westminster Hospital School of Medicine. Used at the Government School of Art, South Kensington. Price 5s.

Artistic Anatomy. The Student's Manual of Artistic Anatomy. With 25 plates of the bones and surface muscles of the human figure; together with a description of the origin, insertion, and uses of the muscles. By W. J. Muckley, Principal of the Manchester School of Art. Used at the Government School of Art, South Kensington. Price 5s. 6d.

Artistic Anatomy. Elementary Anatomical Studies of the Bones and Muscles, for the use of Students and Schools, from the drawings of J. Flaxman, R.A. Lately used as a Text-book of Anatomy in the Art Schools at South Kensington. 20 plates, with Text, price 2s.

Artistic Drawing. Third Grade Perspective, comprising Angular and Oblique Perspective, Shadows and Reflections, specially prepared for the use of Art Students. By H. J. Dennis, Art Master, Lambeth School of Art, Dulwich College, etc. Used at the Government Science and Art Schools. Second edition. In 12 parts, 1s. each, or in 1 vol., half-bound, price 15s.

Artistic Drawing. Second Grade Perspective (Theory and Practice), containing 21 block illustrations, 12 well-executed plates on Parallel and Angular Perspective, and many examination exercises; especially prepared for the use of Art Students. Used at the Government Science and Art Schools. By the same Author. Third thousand, price 2s. 6d.

Artists' Colours. Their Preparation, Uses, etc. By W. J. Muckley. (See Colours.)

Astronomy. The Stars and the Earth; or, Thoughts on Time Space, and Eternity. Revised and enlarged, with Notes by R. A. Proctor, B.A., Hon. Sec. to the Royal Astronomical Society. Thirteenth thousand, price 1s.

Atlases. A Series of Movable Atlases showing the relative position of the several parts of the Human Body by means of superposed coloured plates, from the designs of Prof. G. J. Witkowski. (See Anatomy.)

Botany. Aids to Botany. Outlines of the Elementary Facts including a Description of some of the most important Natural Orders. By C. E. Armand Semple, B.A., M.B. Cantab., M.R.C.P. Lond., Examiner in Arts at the Apothecaries' Hall. Second thousand, price 1s. 6d., cloth, 1s., paper wrapper.

"The student who can commit this to memory will doubtless be proof against pluck."—*Medical Journal.*

Botany. A System of Botanical Analysis, applied to the Diagnosis of British Natural Orders. By Handsel Griffiths, Ph.D., M.R.C.P., late Professor of Chemistry in the Ledwich School of Medicine. Price 1s. 6d.

"The author has placed the student under considerable obligations by his system of botanical analysis."—*Pharmaceutical Journal.*

Brain. The Building of a Brain. By E. H. Clarke, M.D. (author of "Sex in Education"). Price 5s.

"We are much pleased with the little work, which is carefully and elegantly written, and full of sound physiology."—*Lancet.*

Brain. The Brain and Diseases of the Nervous System. 2 vols.

Vol. I. Syphilis of the Brain and Spinal Cord, showing the part which this agent plays in the production of Paralysis, Epilepsy, Insanity, Headache, Neuralgia, Hysteria, and other Mental and Nervous Derangements. By T. Stretch Dowse, M.D., F.R.C.P. Ed., Physician to the Hospital for Epilepsy and Paralysis; formerly Medical Superintendent of the Central London Sick Asylum. Second edition, illustrated, price 7s. 6d.

Vol. II. Neuralgia: its Nature and Curative Treatment. By the same Author. Price 7s. 6d.

Brain. Neurasthenia, or Brain and Nerve Exhaustion. A Paper read before the Medical Society of London. By the same Author. Price 2s. 6d.

Brain. Movable Atlas of the Brain and Skull (Cerebrum, Cerebellum and Medulla Oblongata). By Prof. G. J. Witkowski. (See Anatomy.)

13

Brain. On Mental Capacity in Relation to Insanity, Crime, and Modern Society. By Christopher Smith, M.D. Price 3s. 6d.

Brain. Responsibility and Disease: Moot-points in Jurisprudence about which Medical Men should be well instructed. By J. H. Balfour Browne, Barrister-at-Law, author of "The Medical Jurisprudence of Insanity." Price 2s.

Breath. The Breath, and the Diseases which give it a Fœtid Odour. By J. W. Howe, M.D., Professor of Surgery in the University of New York. Price 4s. 6d.

"The appropriate treatment is pointed out in a manner quite intelligible to the non-medical reader."—*New York Medical Journal.*

Burmah. Our Trip to Burmah, with Notes on the Ethnology, Geography, Botany, Habits and Customs of that Country, by Surgeon-General Gordon, C.B., M.D., Principal Medical Officer, Madras Presidency, Physician to H.M. the Queen. Illustrated with numerous Photographs, Maps, Coloured Plates, and Sketches by native Artists. Price 21s.

"We lay down this book, impressed with its many beauties, its amusing sketches and anecdotes, and its useful and instructive information of that comparatively unknown country."—*The Times.*

"A wonderful book, full of interest, instruction, and amusement."—*Saturday Review.*

"A beautiful and intelligent book for a present."—*Morning Post.*

Case-Books. Students' Case-book. For recording hospital cases as seen, with full instructions for methodising clinical study. Second edition, revised and enlarged by George Brown, M.R.C.S., Gold Medalist, Charing Cross Hospital, late Demonstrator of Anatomy, Westminster Hospital. Price 1s., cloth limp.

Case-Books. Forms for the taking of Aural Cases. By Lennox Browne, F.R.C.S. Ed., Senior Surgeon to the Central London Throat and Ear Hospital. 25 in boards, price 2s.

Forms for the taking of Throat Cases. 25 in boards, price 2s.

Throat and Ear Cases. 50 in boards, combined, price 3s. 6d.

Chemistry. Aids to Chemistry. By C. E. Armand Semple, B.A., M.B. Cantab., M.R.C.P. Lond., Examiner in Arts at the Apothecaries' Hall. Third Thousand.

Parts I. and II.—Inorganic. Price 1s. 6d., each, cloth; 1s. paper wrapper, or in one vol., cloth, 2s. 6d.

Part III.—Organic. Double part, cloth, 2s. 6d.; paper, 2s.

"Students preparing for Matriculation at the London University, and other Examinations, will find it simply invaluable."—*Students' Journal.*

Chemistry. Chemical Tables: Oxides, Sulphides, and Chlorides, with Forms for other Compounds. For the use of Teachers and Students. By Prof. Collenette. Price 6d.

14

Chemistry. Chemical Notes for Pharmaceutical Students, including the Chemistry of the Additions to the Pharmacopœia. By A. Rivers Willson. Price 2s. 6d.

Chemistry. Short Lectures on Experimental Chemistry. Introductory to the general course. By J. Emerson Reynolds, F.R.S., F.C.S., Professor of Chemistry, Royal College of Surgeons, Professor of Analytical Chemistry, and Keeper of the Minerals, Royal Dublin Society. Price 3s. 6d.

Chemistry. An Introduction to Analytical Chemistry for Laboratory Use. By John Muter, Ph.D., M.A., F.C.S., President of the Society of Public Analysts. Third edition, price 7s. 6d.

Chemistry. An Introduction to Pharmaceutical and Medical Chemistry, Theoretical and Practical. With Analytical Tables and copious Index. By the same Author. Price 10s. 6d.

"The book is one of a very useful and original kind, and is brought up to the latest date, tests and processes published only a few months since being described in their proper places."—*Chemical News.*

Chemistry. Chemical Notes and Equations: for the use of Students. By R. Milne Murray, M.A., M.B., C.M. Edin. Price 2s.

Chemistry. Chemistry in its Application to the Arts and Manufactures. A Text-book by Richardson and Watts.

Vol. I.: Parts 1 and 2.—Fuel and its Applications. 433 engravings, and 4 plates. Price £1 16s.

Part 3.—Acids, Alkalies, Salts, Soap, Soda, Chlorine and its Bleaching Compounds, Iodine, Bromine, Alkalimetry, Glycerine, Railway Grease, etc., their Manufacture and Applications, price £1 13s.

Part 4.—Phosphorus, Mineral Waters, Gunpowder, Gun-cotton, Fireworks, Aluminium, Stannates, Tungstates, Chromates and Silicates of Potash and Soda, Lucifer Matches, price £1 1s.

Part 5.—Prussiate of Potash, Oxalic Acid, Tartaric Acid, many tables, plates, and wood engravings, price £1 16s.

Chemistry. Practical Treatise on Acids, Alkalies, and Salts: their Manufacture and Application. In three vols., being Parts III., IV., V. of the previous work, price £4 10s.

Chemistry. The Principles of Theoretical Chemistry, with special reference to the constitution of Chemical Compounds. By Ira Remsen, M.D., Ph.D. Price 6s.

"Worthy of careful perusal."—*New York Medical Record.*

Children. On Tetany in Young Children. By J. Abercrombie, M.D., M.R.C.P. Lond., Medical Registrar to the Hospital for Sick Children. Price 2s.

15

Children. The Feeding and Nursing of. (See Nursing.)

Cholera. Cholera: how to Prevent and Resist it. By Professor von Pettenkofer, University of Munich, President of the Sanitary Department of the German Empire; and Thomas Whiteside Hime, A.B., M.B., Medical Officer of Health for Sheffield, Lecturer on Medicine at the Sheffield School of Medicine. Illustrated with woodcuts and diagram, price 3s. 6d.

Cholera. Notes on the Hygiene of Cholera, for ready reference. Prepared from Official Returns, for the use of Army Medical Officers, Medical Officers of Health, and others. By C. A. Gordon, M.D., C.B., Hon. Physician to the Queen. Price 5s.

Clinical Charts for Recording the Range of Temperature, Pulse, Respiration, History, Progress, and Treatment of Cases, for use in Hospitals and in private practice. By E. W. Moore, M.D., M.R.C.P. Price 1d. each, 9d. per dozen, or mounted, similar to a blotting-pad, in 50, 3s. 6d.; 100, 7s.

Colours. A Hand-book for Painters and Art Students, on the use of Colours, Vehicles, etc. By W. J. Muckley, Principal of the Manchester School of Art (Author of "The Students' Manual of Artistic Anatomy"). Price 3s. 6d.

Consumption. Consumption, as a Contagious Disease, with Treatment: including an Inquiry into the Relative Merits of the Air of Mountains and Plains; to which is prefixed a translation of Cohnheim's Pamphlet. By D. H. Cullimore, M.K.Q.C.P., F.R.C.S.I., Physician North-West London Hospital, formerly Consulting Physician to the King of Burmah; Surgeon H.M. Indian Army. Price 5s.

Consumption. Consumption and its Treatment by the Hypophosphites. By John C. Thorowgood, M.D., F.R.C.P. Lond., Physician to the City of London Hospital for Diseases of the Chest, Victoria Park. Third edition, price 2s. 6d.

Consumption. Consumption, its True Nature and Successful Treatment, with Appendix of Cases. By Godwin Timms, M.D. Lond., M.R.C.P., Senior Physician to the North London Consumption Hospital, Consulting Physician to the Western City Dispensary, etc. Second edition, price 10s. 6d.

Consumption. Phosphates in Nutrition: the Mineral Theory of Consumption and Allied Diseases. By M. F. Anderson, L.R.C.P. Ed., M.R.C.S.E. Price 5s.

"Characterised by a considerable degree of original and painstaking work."—*Medical Press.*

"Certainly deserves the serious attention of all."—*Chemist and Druggist.*

16

Debility. On Tropical Debility, its Causes and Treatment. By Jas. C. Dickinson, M.R.C.S., late of Her Majesty's Bengal Army. Price 1s. 6d.

Deafmutism. On the Education of the Deafmute. By Professor Hartmann. Translated by Dr. Patterson Cassells. (In the Press.)

Deafness. (See Ear.)

Deformities. The Nature and Treatment of Deformities of the Human Body. By Lambert H. Ormsby, M.B. Univ. Dub., Surgeon to the Meath Hospital and County Dublin Infirmary. Crown 8vo., illustrated, price 5s.

Deformities. 1. A Short Sketch of Rational Medical Gymnastics; or, the Movement-Cure. By B. M. Roth, M.D., F.R.C.S. Eng. With thirty-eight engravings, price 1s.

2. The Prevention and Cure of Many Chronic Diseases by Movements. By the same Author. With 90 engravings, price 10s.

3. The Hand-book of the Movement-Cure. By the same Author. With 155 original engravings, price 10s.

4. Contribution to the Hygienic Treatment of Paralysis, and of Paralytic Deformities. By the same Author. With 38 engravings, illustrated by numerous cases, price 3s. 6d.

5. On Paralysis in Infancy, Childhood, and Youth, and on the Prevention and Treatment of Paralytic Deformities. By the same Author. With 45 engravings. Price 3s. 6d.

6. The Prevention of Spinal Deformities, especially of Lateral Curvature, with notes on the causes, the artificial production, and the injurious modes of treatment of these complaints. By the same Author. With 53 engravings, price 3s. 6d.

Diagnosis. Aids to Physical Diagnosis, for the use of Practitioners and Students. By J. C. Thorowgood, M.D., F.R.C.P. Lond., Physician to the City of London Hospital for Diseases of the Chest, and to the West London Hospital, Lecturer on Materia Medica at Middlesex Hospital. Price 1s. and 1s. 6d.

Diagnosis. Aids to Semeiological Diagnosis, for the use of Practitioners and Students. By J. Milner Fothergill, M.D., M.R.C.P. Lond., Assistant Physician to the City of London Hospital for Diseases of the Chest, and to the West London Hospital. Price 1s. and 1s. 6d.

Diphtheria. Diphtheria, its Causes, Pathology, Diagnosis, and Treatment. By R. Hunter Semple, M.D., F.R.C.P. Lond., Physician to the Hospital for Diseases of the Throat and Chest. Second edition, price 2s. 6d.

"It is satisfactory to know that the doctrines laid down by the author, many years ago, do not need negation in any sort of way in the new edition."—*Lancet.*

17

Dissections. The Dissector's Guide, a Manual for the use of Students. By D. J. Cunningham, M.D., Senior Demonstrator of Anatomy, University of Edinburgh. Part I. Upper Limb, Lower Limb, Thorax. Illustrated, price 4s. 6d.

Drugs. The Specific Action of Drugs. An Index to their Therapeutic Value, as deduced from experiments on man and animals. By Alexander G. Burness, M.D., and F. Mavor, President of the Central Lond. Veterinary Society. Price 10s. 6d.

Ear. Aural Surgery. By W. Laidlaw Purves, M.D., Aural Surgeon to Guy's Hospital. (See chapters in Gant's Surgery.)

Ear. Movable Atlas of the Ear. Superposed Coloured Plates. By Prof. G. J. Witkowski, Text by Lennox Browne, F.R.C.S. Ed. Price 7s. 6d. (See Anatomy.)

Ear. Otorrhœa; or, Discharge from the Ears: its Varieties, Causes, Complications, and Treatment. By W. Douglas Hemming, F.R.C.S. Ed. Price 1s.

Ear. Tinnitus Aurium; or, Singing in the Ears: remarks on its Causes and Treatment. By the same Author. Price 1s.

Ear. Text-book of the Diseases of the Ear and adjacent Organs. By Professor Politzer, of Vienna. Translated by James Patterson Cassells, Fellow of the Faculty of Physicians and Surgeons, Glasgow, M.D., and Consulting Physician to the Glasgow Ear Infirmary. Profusely illustrated with coloured plates and woodcuts. (In the Press.)

Ear. The Auriscope, a Hand-book of Aural Diagnosis. By J. Patterson Cassells, M.D. *Shortly.*

Ear. Clinical Aural Surgery, a Practical Treatise on Diseases of the Ear in Infancy, Childhood and Adult Life. *Shortly.*

Ethnology. The History and Genealogy of the Human Race from the Creation; showing how the nations of the world can be traced from the sons and grandsons of Noah. By J. T. Painter. Price 3s. 6d.

Examinations. A Guide to the Examinations at the Royal College of Surgeons of England for the Diplomas of Member and Fellow, with Examination Papers. Third edition, revised and enlarged, price 3s. 6d.

"In truth a most useful Guide to the Examinations."—*Guy's Hospital Gazette.*

Examinations. Aids to Examinations. By W. Douglas Hemming, F.R.C.S. Ed. Being Questions and Answers on Materia Medica, Medicine, Midwifery, Pathology, and Forensic Medicine. Price 1s. 6d. cloth, 1s. paper wrapper.

Eye. A Manual of Examination of the Eyes. By Professor C. Landolt, of Paris. Translated, with the Author's permission and revision, by Swan M. Burnett, M.D. Price 12s. 6d.

"For those who have a taste for examining Eyes, this will prove most helpful."—*Lancet.*

"The author gives with the greatest care and minuteness his methods and results, which render the book an eminently valuable one for practitioners."—*Medical Press.*

18

Eye. The Cure of Cataract and other Eye Affections. By Jabez Hogg, M.R.C.S., Consulting Surgeon to the Royal Westminster Ophthalmic Hospital, Ophthalmic Surgeon to the Royal Masonic Institutions. Price 2s. 6d.

Eye. On Impairment or Loss of Vision from Spinal Concussion or Shock. By the same Author. Price 1s. 6d.

Eye. The Functions of Vision and its Anomalies. By Dr. Giraud-Teulon, Member of the Academie de Medicine. Translated from the Second French Edition, by Lloyd Owen, F.R.C.S.I., Surgeon to the Birmingham and Midland Eye Hospital, Ophthalmic Surgeon to the Free Hospital for Sick Children, Birmingham. Illustrated, price 5s.

Eye. Movable Atlas of the Eye and the Mechanism of Vision. By Prof. G. J. Witkowski. Text by Hy. Power, M.B., F.R.C.S., Senior Ophthalmic Surgeon to, and Lecturer on Ophthalmic Surgery at, St. Bartholomew's Hospital, Senior Surgeon to the Royal Westminster Ophthalmic Hospital. Price 7s. 6d. (See Anatomy.)

Fever. How to Avoid Typhoid Fever and Allied Diseases, with Plain Rules on House Drainage, etc. By Arthur H. Downes, M.B., M.D., Medical Officer of Health for the Chelmsford District. Price 1s.

Food. Food; its Varieties, Chemical Composition, Nutritive Value, Comparative Digestibility, Physical Functions and Uses, Preparation, Preservation, Adulterations, etc. By the late Henry Letheby, M.B., M.A., Ph.D., etc. Second edition, enlarged, price 5s.

"Dr. Letheby's position and authority on the subject of food is so pre-eminent, that a book from his pen is above criticism."—*Lancet.*

"Either as a text-book for schools or as a household guide, it is excellently adapted."—*Public Opinion.*

Forensic Medicine. Aids to Forensic Medicine and Toxicology. By W. Douglas Hemming, F.R.C.S. Ed. Second thousand, price 1s. 6d. cloth, 1s. paper wrapper.

"We have no hesitation in recommending Mr. Hemming's book."—*Lancet.*

Geology. Field Geology, with a Section on Palæontology. By W. Hy. Penning, F.G.S., of H.M. Geological Survey, and A. J. Jukes-Browne, B.A., F.G.S., of H.M. Geological Survey. Illustrated with woodcuts and coloured map. Second edition, revised and enlarged, price 7s. 6d.

"Satisfies a want which has long been felt and frequently expressed."—*Nature.*

"Others have taught us the principles of the science, but Mr. Penning, as an accomplished field-geologist, introduces us to the practice."—*The Academy.*

Geology. Engineering Geology. By the same Author. Illustrated with coloured map and woodcuts, price 3s. 6d.

"A full and lucid description of surveying and mapping, the diagnosing of the various minerals met with, the value of sites and rocks for engineering operations, etc."—*Popular Science Review.*

19

Gout. On the Tonic Treatment of Gout. With Cases. By James C. Dickinson, M.R.C.S., late of H.M.'s Bengal Army. Second edition, price 3s. 6d.

"A thorough and practical work."—*Public Opinion.*

Gout. Suppressed Gout: its Dangers and Treatment; with an Appendix on the Uses of the Vals Waters. By the same Author. Price 2s.

Hair. The Hair: its Growth, Care, Diseases, and Treatment; with Historical Chapters on Fashions in Hair and Beards from the Assyrian to Modern Times. By C. H. Leonard, M.A., M.D. With 116 engravings, price 7s. 6d.

"Is entertaining reading, will afford many useful hints to the practitioner, and be much appreciated by the public, especially the fashionable portion of it."—*Lancet.*

Hay Fever: Its Causes, Treatment, and Effective Prevention; Experimental Researches. By Chas. Harrison Blackley, M.D.

Second edition, revised and enlarged, price 10s. 6d.

"A piece of real honest work, original and instructive, and will well repay perusal."—*Lancet.*

"The treatise before us is one of the fullest that we are acquainted with on this subject; we recommend it cordially to all who may wish for a practical work on this once mysterious disease."—*Medical Times.*

Heart. On Insufficiency of Aortic Valves in Connection with Sudden Death: with Notes, Historical and Critical. By John Cockle, A.M., M.D., F.R.C.P., Physician to the Royal Free Hospital, late President of the Medical Society of London. Second edition, price 2s. 6d.

Heart. Contributions to Cardiac Pathology. By the same Author. Price 2s. 6d.

Heart. An Essay on Fatty Heart. By Henry Kennedy, A.B., M.B. Dub. Univ., Physician to the Whitworth Hospitals. Price 3s. 6d.

"We have no hesitation in recommending it as a most valuable contribution to the literature of the all-important subject of which it treats."—*Medical Press and Circular.*

Histology. Introduction to Practical Histology. By George Thin, M.D. Price 5s.

"No more valuable text-book for the student will be found, nor one containing a greater amount of useful information."—*Medical Press.*

Hydrophobia. The Nature and Treatment of Rabies or Hydrophobia, and those Diseases resembling it. Report of the Special Commission appointed by the *Medical Press and Circular*, with valuable additions. By T. M. Dolan, L.R.C.P., F.R.C.S. Ed., and George Fleming, F.R.C.V.S. Second edition, price 5s.

"The most valuable and complete treatise on the subject; one which we can highly recommend."—*Veterinary Journal.*

"This laborious work is a credit alike to the writers, and the journal which first published it."—*The Doctor.*

Hygiene. Lessons in Military Hygiene and Surgery, from the Franco-Prussian War. Reports prepared while on Special Service with the French Army in Paris, on behalf of Her Majesty's Government. By Surgeon-General Gordon, M.D., C.B., Hon. Physician to the Queen. Illustrated, price 10s. 6d.

"A treatise of exceptional merit, drawn from personal experiences in the greatest war of modern times."—*Army and Navy Gazette.*

20

Hygiene. A Manual of Sanitation; or, First Help in Sickness and when Wounded. A pocket companion for officers and privates in the army or volunteer forces in peace and in war. By the same Author. Second edition, price, cloth 2s. 6d., or cheap edition, paper wrapper 1s.

"It is a most useful and practical manual, and, as the instructions are simple and reliable, it should be placed in the hands of officers and men alike."—*Medical Press.*

Hygiene. A Manual of Hygiene, Public and Private, and Compendium of Sanitary Laws, for the information and guidance of Public Health Authorities and Sanitarians generally. By Chas. A. Cameron, M.D., F.R.C.S., Professor of Hygiene, Royal College of Surgeons, Medical Officer of Health and Public Analyst, Dublin. Price 10s. 6d.

"By far the most comprehensive work on hygiene for health officers and others, which we have met with."—*Pharmaceutical Journal.*

Hygiene. On Disease Prevention. A Practical Treatise on Disinfection. By the same Author. Price 6d.

"Contains practical directions for disinfecting rooms, clothing, bedding, etc., with chapters on vaccination, water impurities, and other important sanitary matters."—*Sanitary Review.*

Hygiene. On Vitiated Air. A Paper read before the Association of Medical Officers of Health. By C. Meymott Tidy, M.B., F.C.S., Professor of Chemistry and Medical Jurisprudence in the London Hospital. Price 6d.

Hygiene. Short Lectures on Sanitary Subjects. By Richard J. Halton, L.K.Q.C.P., L.R.C.P. Ed., L.R.C.S.I., etc., Medical Officer of Health to Kells. Price 5s.

"A book well adapted to popular reading, and replete with sound knowledge promotive of good health and long life."—*Sanitarian.*

Hygiene. Nature's Hygiene: A Series of Essays on Popular Scientific Subjects, with special reference to the Eucalyptus and the Pine. By C. T. Kingzett, F.I.C., F.C.S. Demy 8vo., price 7s. 6d.

"These highly interesting and instructive pages."—*Standard.*

"Scientific, yet withal most interesting reading. It were well if the public would study it themselves."—*Graphic.*

Hygiene. A Manual of Naval Hygiene, with Instructions and Hints on the Preservation of Health and the Prevention of Disease on board Ship. By Joseph Wilson, M.D., Medical Director of the United States Navy. Second edition, price 10s. 6d.

"No ship should be allowed to leave port without this valuable manual; yachtsmen will also find it a most readable and useful companion."—*Medical Press.*

India. Experiences of an Army Surgeon in India. By Surgeon-General Gordon, M.D., C.B., Hon. Physician to the Queen, A Concise Account of the Treatment of the Wounds, Injuries, and Diseases incidental to a Residence in that Country. Price 3s. 6d.

Kidneys. Bright's Disease of the Kidneys. By J. M. Charcot, Professor in the Faculty of Medicine, Paris. Translated by H. B. Millard, M.D., A.M. Revised by the Author, with coloured plates, price 7s. 6d.

"We doubt very much if there exists in the English language any monograph in which the various forms are so accurately and concisely described."—*Medical Press.*

21

Life. (See Theories of Life.)

Lunacy. Handbook for Attendants on the Insane, their duties and liabilities; instructions for the management, artificial feeding, and mechanical restraint of the insane; legal documents required for their confinement, etc. By L. S. Forbes Winslow, M.B., D.C.L. Oxon.; M.R.C.P.; Lecturer on Mental Diseases, Charing Cross Hospital (Editor of *The Journal of Psychological Medicine*). Price 1s.

Lunacy. Manual of Lunacy. A Handbook relating to the Legal care and treatment of the Insane. By the same Author. Price 12s. 6d.

"A comprehensive digest of every subject connected with the legal care of the insane."—*Medical Times.*

Lunacy. A Lunacy Chart: being a Synopsis of the Lunacy Acts, and having special reference to the management and care of persons of Unsound Mind. By the same Author. Price 1s. 6d., varnished and mounted on canvas and rollers, 4s. 6d.

Lunacy. Spiritualistic Madness. By the same Author. Price 1s.

Materia Medica. Aids to Materia Medica and Therapeutics. Part I.—The Non-metallic and Metallic Elements, Alcoholic and Ethereal Preparations, etc. By C. E. Armand Semple, B.A.,

M.B. Cantab., M.R.C.P. Lond., Examiner in Arts at the Apothecaries' Hall. Price, cloth 1s. 6d., paper wrapper 1s.

Part II.—The Vegetable and Animal Substances. Double Part, price, cloth 2s. 6d., paper 2s.

Materia Medica. Note-Book of Materia Medica and Therapeutics. By R. E. Scoresby-Jackson, M.D., F.R.S. Revised by Angus Macdonald, M.A., F.R.S. (New edition, in the Press.)

"A work we can recommend with the utmost confidence."—*Students' Journal.*

Materia Medica. A Key to Organic Materia Medica. By John Muter, Ph.D., M.A., F.C.S., President of the Society of Public Analysts. Third edition, price 12s. 6d.

Materia Medica and Pharmacy. A Text-Book for Medical and Pharmaceutical Students preparing for Examination. By W. Handsel Griffiths, Ph.D., F.C.S., F.R.C.P. Ed. Edited, and in part written, by George F. Duffey, M.D. Dub., Fellow and Examiner K.Q.C.P., Examiner in Materia Medica, Queen's University of Ireland, Lecturer on Materia Medica in the Carmichael College of Medicine, etc. Price 9s.

"A book of great value to the profession.... Will undoubtedly become a standard text-book on Materia Medica."—*Edinburgh Medical Journal.*

"Conveys a large amount of reliable information in a clear and attractive form."—*Dublin Journal of Medical Science.*

"One of the ablest, if not the best, work on the subject in the English language."—*Medical Press and Circular.*

22

Medical Education. Medical Education and Medical Organization. The Hunterian Oration for 1880. By Walter Rivington, B.A., M.B., F.R.C.S., Surgeon to the London Hospital, Examiner in Anatomy and Physiology, Royal College of Surgeons, England. Price 1s.

Medical Profession. The Medical Profession: being the Essay to which was awarded the First Carmichael Prize of £200 by the Council of the Royal College of Surgeons, Ireland, 1879. By Walter Rivington, B.A., M.B., F.R.C.S., Surgeon to the London Hospital, Examiner in Anatomy and Physiology, Royal College of Surgeons, England. Price 6s.

Medical Profession. The Medical Profession in the Three Kingdoms in 1879: being the Essay to which was awarded the Second Carmichael Prize of £100. By Thomas Laffan, L.K.Q.C.P.I., M.R.C.S. Ed., Physician to the Cashel Union and Fever Hospitals. Price 4s.

Medical Profession. Medical Men and Manners of the Nineteenth Century. By a Physician. Third Thousand, price 3s.

"At times scathing, at others amusing, the author is never dull, and writes withal, as one who knows from experience the many blots on our system, and honestly tries to remedy them."—*Medical Press.*

"A most amusing satire, brimful of humour even when dealing with unpleasant facts."—*Students' Journal.*

Medical Reform. The General Medical Council: Whom it represents, and How it should be re-constructed. By Archibald Hamilton Jacob, M.D. Dub., F.R.C.S., Member of Council in the Royal College of Surgeons, Ireland, Surgeon-Oculist to His Excellency the Lord Lieutenant of Ireland. Price 1s.

Medical Reform. The Medical Acts Amendment Bill and Medical Reform. A Paper read before the Abernethian Society at St. Bartholomew's Hospital. By W. E. Steavenson, M.B. Cantab., M.R.C.S. Ed. Price 1s.

Medicine. Aids to Medicine. Part I.—General Diseases. Diseases of the Lungs, Heart, and Liver. By C. E. Armand Semple, B.A., M.B. Cantab., M.R.C.P. Lond. Price 1s. 6d.

Part II.—Pathology of the Urine, Diseases of the Kidneys, Pancreas, Spleen, Stomach, Peritoneum, Throat, and Œsophagus. Price 1s. 6d. cloth, 1s. paper wrapper.

Medicine. A Chronology of Medicine from the Earliest Times. By J. Morgan Richards. Price 10s. 6d.

Medicine. Essays on Conservative Medicine, and kindred topics. By Austin Flint, M.D., Professor of the Principles and Practice of Medicine in Bellevue Hosp. Medical College, New York. Price 5s.

23

Medicine>. Handbook of Popular Medicine for family instruction and reference; for colonists, travellers and others out of reach of medical aid. By G. H. Napheys, A.M., M.D. With movable plate and 100 illustrations. Price 6s.

"We have rarely read any form of domestic medicine so simple, yet reliable."—*Public Opinion.*

Medico-Military Services. A Contribution to the Medical History of our West African Campaigns, by Surgeon-Major Albert A. Gore, M.D., Sanitary Officer on the Staff. Price 10s. 6d.

"Dr. Gore has given us a most interesting record of a series of stirring events in which he took an active part, and of elaborate precautions for the maintenance of health."—*Medical Press.*

Medico-Military Services. Our Services under the Crown. A Historical Sketch of the Army Medical Staff. By the same author. Price 6s.

Military Surgery. Lessons in Hygiene and Surgery, from the Franco-Prussian War. Prepared while on Special Service with the French Army in Paris, on behalf of Her Majesty's Government. By Surgeon-General C. Gordon, M.D., C.B., Physician to Her Majesty the Queen. Illustrated, price 10s. 6d.

Mind. The Training of the Mind for the Study of Medicine. A Lecture delivered at St. George's Hospital. By Robert Brudenell Carter, F.R.C.S., Surgeon to the Hospital. Price 1s.

"A remarkable address."—*The Lancet.*

"No one can read it without learning and profiting much."—*Students' Journal.*

Morals. Cheerful Words: Short Sermons for Asylums, Hospitals, Gaols, and other Public Institutions. By Dignitaries of the Church, and Clergymen. Edited by Wm. Hyslop, Superintendent of Stretton House Asylum. Vols. I., II., price 5s. each.

Morals. A Physician's Sermon to Young Men. By William Pratt, M.A., M.D., etc. Second thousand, price 1s.

"The delicate topic is handled wisely, judiciously, and religiously, as well as very plainly."—*The Guardian.*

Morals. Revelations of Quacks and Quackery. A Directory of the London and Provincial Quack Doctors; with Facts and Cases in Illustration of their Nefarious Practices. By "Detector." Twenty-fifth thousand, price 1s. 6d.

Natural History. Contributions to Natural History, and papers on other subjects. By Jas. Simson (Author of "History of the Gipsies"). Second edition, price 6s.

Neuralgia. Its Nature, Causes, and Curative Treatment. By Thos. Stretch Dowse, M.D., F.R.C.P. Ed., Physician to the Hospital for Epilepsy and Paralysis, formerly Medical Superintendent of the Central London Sick Asylum. Price 7s. 6d.

Nursing. Hints for Hospital Nurses. By Rachel Williams, of St. Mary's Hospital, London, and the Edinburgh Royal Infirmary, and Alice Fisher, of the Newcastle-on-Tyne Fever Hospital. Price 2s. 6d.

24

Nursing. How to Feed an Infant. With an Appendix on the Common Ailments of Infancy, with their Hygienic and Curative Treatment. By Benson Baker, M.D. Price 1s. 6d.

"Popularly written, and sensible in the highest degree, its widespread perusal would help to bring about a more rational system of bringing up infants."—*Graphic.*

"Based upon the wide and practical experience of the Author."—*Society.*

Nursing. How to bring up Children by Hand. By J. Foster Palmer, L.R.C.P. Price 6d.

Nursing. Practical Guide for the Young Mother. From the French of Dr. Brochard, Director-General of Nurseries and Crêches, with Notes and Hints by a London Physician. Price 2s.

Nursing. The Child, and How to Nurse it. By Alex. Milne, M.D., Vice-President of the Obstetrical Society of Edinburgh. Price 2s. 6d.

Obstetrics. Lessons in Gynæcology and Obstetrics. By William Goodell, A.M., M.D., Professor of Clinical Gynæcology in the University of Pennsylvania. Second edition, with ninety-two illustrations, price 18s.

Obstetrics. The Therapeutics of Gynæcology and Obstetrics, comprising the Medical, Dietetic and Hygienic Treatment of Diseases of Women, as set forth by distinguished contemporary Specialists. Edited by William B. Atkinson, A.M., M.D. Price 15s.

Obstetrics. Obstetrics and Diseases of Women. By Robert Barnes, M.D., F.R.C.P. Lond., Obstetric Physician and Lecturer on Diseases of Women, St. George's Hospital (see chapters in Gant's Surgery).

Obstetrics. On Fibrous Tumours of the Womb: Points connected with their Pathology, Diagnosis and Treatment. Being the Lettsomian Lectures delivered before the Medical Society of London. By C. H. F. Routh, M.D., M.R.C.P. Lond., Senior Physician to the Samaritan Hospital for Women. Price 3s. 6d.

Osteology. Osteology for Students, with Atlas of Plates. By Arthur Trehern Norton, F.R.C.S., Surgeon to, and Lecturer on Surgery at, St. Mary's Hospital. Atlas and Text in one volume, 7s. 6d.; in two volumes, 8s. 6d.

"The handiest and most complete handbook of Osteology."—*The Lancet.*

Overwork. Overwork and Premature Mental Decay: its Treatment. By C. H. F. Routh, M.D., M.R.C.P. Lond., Senior Physician to the Samaritan Hospital for Women and Children. Third edition, price 2s. 6d.

Palæontology. A Treatise on Palæontology. By A. J. Jukes-Browne, B.A., F.G.S., of Her Majesty's Geological Survey (see Field Geology and Palæontology, by Penning and Jukes-Browne).

25

Pharmacy. A Treatise on Pharmacy. A Text-book for Students, and a Guide for the Physician and Pharmacist. By Edward Parrish. Fourth edition, enlarged and revised by T. S. Wiegand, F.C.S. With 280 illustrations, half-bound morocco, price 30s.

"There is nothing to equal Parrish's Pharmacy in this on any other language."—*Pharmaceutical Journal.*

Physiological Laboratory. A Manual for the Physiological Laboratory. By Vincent Harris, M.D., M.R.C.P. Lond., Demonstrator of Physiology at St. Bartholomew's Hospital, and D'Arcy Power, B.A. Oxon., Assistant Demonstrator. Price 3s. 6d.

"A book which should be in every student's hands."—*Medical Press.*

Physiology. Aids to Physiology. By B. Thompson Lowne, F.R.C.S., Arris and Gale Lecturer and Examiner in Physiology, Royal College of Surgeons of England. Price 2s. 6d. cloth, 2s. paper wrapper.

"As 'aids' and not substitutes, they will prove of real value to students."—*Medical Press.*

"Certainly one of the best of the now popular 'Aid Series.'"—*Students' Journal.*

Physiology. Manual of Physiology. By Professors Kuss and Duval, of Strasbourg. Translated by Professor Amory, M.D. Illustrated with 150 engravings, price 10s. 6d.

"The best Students' Manual we have seen."—*Medico-Chirurgical Review.*

"One of the best in the English language."—*Medical Press.*

Physiology. Movable Atlases of Anatomy and Physiology. Superposed coloured plates. By Prof. G. J. Witkowski. A Companion and Supplement to every work on the subject. (See Anatomy.)

Physiology. The Physiology of Intestinal Obstruction and Constipation. By C. J. Harris, M.R.C.S. Price 1s.

Physiology. The Physiologist in the Household. By J. Milner Fothergill, M.D., M.R.C.P., Lond. Part I. Adolescence. Price 1s.

Population. On the Evils, Moral and Physical, likely to follow, if practices, intended to act as checks to population, be not strongly discouraged and condemned. Read at the Annual Meeting of the British Medical Association, with the discussion thereon. Second thousand, price 1s.

Posology. Posological Tables: a Classified Chart of Diseases, showing at a glance the Dose of every Officinal Substance and Preparation. For the use of Practitioners and Students. By Handsel Griffiths, Ph.D., L.R.C.P., etc., late Professor of Chemistry, Ledwich School of Medicine. Fourth edition, price 1s.

Posology. The Pharmacopœial Companion to the Visiting List. A Posological Table of all the Medicines of the British Pharmacopœia, arranged according to their action. By R. T. H. Bartley, M.D., M.B. Lond., Surgeon to the Bristol Eye Hospital. Second edition, price 6d.

Post-Mortems. Hand-book of Post-Mortem Examinations, and of Morbid Anatomy. By Francis Delafield, M.D., Curator to Bellevue Hospital, New York. Price 15s.

Protoplasm. See Theories of Life.

Sewage. The Sewage Question: Reports upon the Principal Sewage Farms and Works of the Kingdom, with Notes and Chemical Analyses. By the late Dr. Letheby. Price 4s. 6d.

"These Reports will dissipate obscurity, and, by placing the subject in a proper light, will enable local authorities, and others interested in the matter, to perceive the actual truths of the question, and to apply them practically."

Skin. Diseases of the Skin. By Erasmus Wilson, F.R.S., F.R.C.S., Vice-President of the Royal College of Surgeons, England. (See chapters in Gant's "Surgery").

Skin. Some Diseases of the Skin which are produced by derangements of the Nervous System. By T. Stretch Dowse, M.D., F.R.C.P. Ed., Physician to the Hospital for Paralysis and Epilepsy, and Physician, Skin Department, Charing Cross Hospital. Price 2s.

Skin. Lectures on Ring-worm and other Diseases of the Skin, due to Vegetoid Parasites. By Jas. Startin, M.R.C.S. Price 1s.

Sphygmograph. The Use of the Sphygmograph in Surgery. By F. A. Mahomed, M.D., M.R.C.P. Lond., Medical Registrar, Guy's Hospital. (See chapter in Gant's "Surgery.")

Surgery. The Science and Practice of Surgery, being a Complete Text-book. With special chapters by

Wm. Adams, F.R.C.S., Deformities.
Robt. Barnes, M.D., F.R.C.P., Obstetrics.
Morell Mackenzie, M.D., The Throat.
F. A. Mahomed, M.D., The Sphygmograph.
Hy. Power, F.R.C.S., Ophthalmic Surgery.
Laidlaw Purves, M.D., Aural Surgery.
C. S. Tomes, M.A., Oxon, F.R.S., Dental Surgery
Prof. Erasmus Wilson, F.R.S., The Skin.

By Frederick J. Gant, F.R.C.S., President of the Medical Society of London, Senior Surgeon to the Royal Free Hospital. Second edition, illustrated by nearly 1000 engravings, new and original, in 2 vols., price 31s. 6d.

"Gant's able and laborious work must be commended."—*The Lancet.*

"Does credit to the author's thorough surgical knowledge."—*British Medical Journal.*

"Will become one of the most popular Surgical Text-books in the English language."—*Medical Press.*

"A very complete and trustworthy guide to practice."—*Medical Times.*

Surgery. Aids to Surgery. By George Brown, M.R.C.S., Gold Medalist, Charing Cross Hospital, Author of "Aids to Anatomy." Price 1s. 6d. cloth, 1s. paper wrapper.

Surgery. The Text-book of Operative Surgery. From the French of Professors Claude Bernard and Huette. With 88 plates. Text edited and re-written, by Arthur Trehern Norton, F.R.C.S., Surgeon to, and Lecturer on Surgery at, St, Mary's Hospital. Price, plain, 25s.; coloured, half-calf, 50s.

"Of the highest merit as a guide to operative surgery."—*Students' Journal.*

27

Surgery. Abstracts of Surgical Principles for Medical Students. By Thos. Annandale, F.R.C.S., F.R.S., Surgeon to, and Lecturer on Surgery at, Royal Infirmary, Edinburgh. Price 7s. 6d.

Surgery. A Manual of the Operations of Surgery, for the use of Senior Students, etc. By Joseph Bell, F.R.C.S., Lecturer on Surgery, Royal Infirmary, Edinburgh. Third edition, price 6s,

Teeth. Dental Surgery. By Chas. S. Tomes, M.A. Oxon, E.R.S. (See chapters in Gant's "Surgery.")

Teeth. Movable Atlas of the Teeth and Ear. By Professor Witkowski. (See Anatomy.)

Teeth. The Dental Student's Note-Book. By Oakley Coles, L.D.S. Second thousand, price 2s. 6d.

Theories of Disease. The Germ Theories of Infectious Diseases. By John Drysdale, M.D., F.R.M.S., President of the Liverpool Microscopical Society. Price 1s.

Theories of Disease. A Parasitic or Germ Theory of Disease: the Skin, Eye, and other affections. By Jabez Hogg, M.R.C.S., Consulting Surgeon to the Royal Westminster Ophthalmic Hospital. Second edition, price 2s. 6d.

Theories of Life. The Protoplasmic Theory of Life. Containing the Latest Researches on the subject. By John Drysdale, M.D., F.R.M.S., President of the Liverpool Microscopical Society. Price 5s.

"Subjects beyond the pale of precise knowledge are treated of in a manner which will quite repay perusal."—*Nature.*

Theories of Life. Life and the Equivalence of Force. By the same Author.

Part I. Historical Notice of the Discovery of the Law of Equivalence of Force. Price 1s.

Part II. Nature of Force and Life: containing the Harmony of Fletcher and Beale. Price 1s. 6d.

"We cannot part from this work without praising the calm and excellent spirit in which the subject is bandied."—*The Examiner.*

Theories Of Life. Can we Prolong Life? An Enquiry into the Causes of Premature Old Age and Death. By C. W. de Lacy Evans, M.R.C.S. Price 5s.

"A good account of the somatic changes which occur with the advance of age."—*The Lancet.*

"This is a very ingenious and interesting book."—*Chemist and Druggist.*

Therapeutics. Modern Medical Therapeutics. A compendium of recent Formula and Specific Therapeutical directions, from the practice of eminent Contemporary Physicians, English, American, and Foreign. Edited by G. H. Napheys, A.M., M.D. Seventh edition, price 18s.

"No one who carefully peruses this work can feel surprised at the demand for it; edition after edition sells with great rapidity."—*Medical Press.*

"A summary of the best modes of treatment."—*Practitioner.*

"The volume will supply what many practitioners are often anxious to possess for reference in the practice of their art."—*Glasgow Medical Journal.*

28

Therapeutics. Modern Surgical Therapeutics. A Compendium of the most recent Formulæ, and specific Therapeutical directions; from the Practice of eminent contemporary Physicians and Surgeons, English, American, and Foreign. Edited by G. H. Napheys, A.M., M.D. Sixth edition, price 18s.

"Of much value to the surgeon and general practitioner."—*New York Medical Journal.*

"Invaluable to every practising physician."—*New York Medical Record.*

"All that is in the book is good."—*Philadelphia Medical Times.*

Therapeutics. Aids to Rational Therapeutics, for the guidance of Practitioners and Senior Students. By J. Milner Fothergill, M.D. Price 2s., paper wrapper; 2s. 6d., cloth.

Therapeutics. The Therapeutics of Gynæcology and Obstetrics, comprising the Medical, Dietetic and Hygienic Treatment of Diseases of Women as set forth by Contemporary Specialists. Edited by W. B. Atkinson, A.M., M.D. Price 15s. (See Obstetrics.)

Throat. Movable Atlas of the Throat, and the Mechanism of Voice, Speech, and Taste. By Prof. Witkowski. (See Anatomy.)

Throat. Diseases of the Throat. By Morell Mackenzie, M.D. (See chapters in Gant's "Surgery.")

Throat. The Throat and its Diseases. A Practical Guide to Diagnosis and Treatment. With 100 typical illustrations in chromo-lithography (seven colours) and 50 wood engravings, designed and executed by the Author, Lennox Browne, F.R.C.S. Ed., Senior Surgeon to the Central London Throat and Ear Hospital, Surgeon and Aural Surgeon to the Royal Society of Musicians, etc. Second Edition, price 18s.

Throat. Affections of the Throat and Larynx. By Arthur Trehern Norton, F.R.C.S., Surgeon to St. Mary's Hospital. Second edition, illustrated, price 6s.

"Short, simple, and thoroughly practical instruction."—*Medical Times.*

Throat. Lessons in Laryngoscopy and Rhinoscopy: including the Diagnosis and Treatment of Diseases of the Throat and Nose. Illustrated with hand-coloured plates and woodcuts. By Prosser James, M.D., M.R.C.P., Lecturer on Materia Medica and Therapeutics at the London Hospital, Physician to the Hospital for Diseases of the Throat, etc. Third edition, price 5s. 6d.

Urine. The Urine. A Guide to its Practical Examination. By Prof. J. Tyson, M.D., Professor of Morbid Anatomy in the University of Pennsylvania, and President of the Pathological Society of Philadelphia. With numerous illustrations, price 5s.

29

Veterinary. A Text-book of Veterinary Obstetrics, including the diseases and accidents incidental to pregnancy, parturition, and early age in the Domesticated Animals. By George Fleming, F.R.C.V.S., F.G.S., President of the Royal Veterinary College, (Editor of "The Veterinary Journal.") Price 30s. cloth, copiously illustrated.

"Every page impresses upon the reader the highest sense of the exceptional learning and consummate skill of the author."—*The Lancet.*

"Has filled up a void in a more satisfactory and complete way than any other member of his profession could have done."—*The Field.*

"No man who makes any pretensions to Veterinary Science or Stock-breeding can dispense with this work."—*Live Stock Journal.*

Veterinary. A Text-book of Veterinary Pathology and Practical Therapeutics. By the same Author. (In preparation.)

Veterinary. Animal Plagues, their History, Nature, and Treatment. By the same Author. Price 15s.

Veterinary. The Contagious Diseases of Animals: their influence on the wealth and health of the nation. Read before the Society of Arts. By the same Author. Price 6d.

Veterinary. A Manual of Veterinary Sanitary Science and Police, embracing the nature, causes, and symptoms of Diseases in Cattle, their prevention, treatment, etc. By the same Author. 2 vols., price 36s.

Veterinary. Practical Horse-Shoeing. By the same Author. Third edition, price 2s.

Veterinary. A Manual of Operative Veterinary Surgery. By the same Author. *Shortly.*

Veterinary. The Principles and Practice of Veterinary Surgery; embracing the Surgical Pathology of all the Domesticated Animals. By Wm. Williams, F.R.C.V.S., Principal and Professor of Veterinary Medicine and Surgery at the New Veterinary College, Edinburgh. With 140 illustrations. Third edition, price 30s.

Veterinary. The Principles and Practice of Veterinary Medicine. By the same Author. Second edition, with plates, price 30s.

Veterinary. A Text-book on the Examination of Horses as to Soundness. A course of Lectures delivered at the Royal Veterinary College, Edinburgh. By Professor Fearnley. With an Appendix on the Law of Horses and Warranty. Illustrated, price 7s. 6d.

Veterinary. Lessons in Horse-Judging, with instructions on the Summering of Hunters. By the same Author. Illustrated, price 4s.

30

Veterinary. The Four Bovine Scourges: Pleuroneumonia, Foot and Mouth Disease, Cattle Plague, and Tubercle; with an Appendix on the Inspection of Live Animals and Meat. By Thos. Walley, Principal and Professor of Veterinary Medicine and Surgery, Edinburgh Royal Veterinary College. Price 16s.

Veterinary. The Management and Diseases of the Dog. By J. W. Hill, F.R.C.V.S. Copiously illustrated, price 10s. 6d.

"Contains much valuable information."—*The Field.*

"An excellent and complete manual."—*The Standard.*

Veterinary. Principles and Practice of Bovine Medicine and Surgery. By the same Author. Copiously illustrated. (In the Press.)

Veterinary. The Diseases of Live Stock, and their most Efficient Remedies; including Horses, Cattle, Sheep, and Swine: being a Popular Treatise, giving in brief and plain language a description of all the usual diseases to which these animals are liable, and the most successful treatment of English, American, and Continental Veterinarians. By Lloyd V. Tellor, M.D., V.S. Price 10s. 6d.

Veterinary. Strangeway's Veterinary Anatomy. Revised and Edited by J. Vaughan, F.L.S., F.Z.S. Second edition, price 24s.

Veterinary. Anatomical Outlines of the Horse. By J. A. McBride, Ph.D., M.R.C.V.S. Second edition. Revised and enlarged by T. Walter Mayer, F.R.C.V.S., Examiner at the Royal Veterinary College. Illustrated, price 8s. 6d.

Veterinary. Horses: their Rational Treatment, and the Causes of their Premature Decay. By "Amateur." Price 5s.

Veterinary. An Abridgment of the Above. By the same Author. Price 1s.

The Philosophy of Voice. Showing the right and wrong Action of the Breath and Vocal Cords in the Production of Articulate Speech and Song. By Charles Lunn. Fourth Edition. Price 1s. 6d.

PERIODICAL PUBLICATIONS.

The Medical Press and Circular. Established 1838. Published every Wednesday in London, Dublin, and Edinburgh. One of the oldest and most influential Medical Journals. Price 5d.; £1 1s. per annum, post free, in advance.

The Student's Journal and Hospital Gazette. A Fortnightly Review of Medicine, Surgery, and the Collateral Sciences. The only Paper that represents the whole body of Medical Students. Price 4d.; 7s. 6d. per annum, prepaid.

31

The Veterinary Journal, and Annals of Comparative Pathology. Edited by George Fleming, F.R.C.V.S., President of the Royal College of Veterinary Surgeons. Monthly, price 1s. 6d.; 18s. per annum, prepaid.

The Analyst. The Official Organ of "The Society of Public Analysts." The best Journal for Medical Officers of Health, Sanitarians, and those interested in the purity of Food, Drugs, &c., monthly. Price 6d. 5s. per annum, if paid in advance.

Quarterly Journal of Inebriety. Published under the auspices of The American Association for the Cure of Inebriates. Price, 2s. 6d. each; 10s. per annum, post free.

The Journal of Psychological Medicine and Mental Pathology. Edited by Lyttleton S. Forbes Winslow, M.B., D.C.L. Oxon., Lecturer on Mental Diseases. Charing Cross Hospital. Half-yearly, April and October, price 3s. 6d.; 7s. per annum, post free, prepaid.

DIRECTORIES.

The Irish Medical Directory (Annual). A Directory of the Profession in Ireland; their Residences and Qualifications; the Public Offices which they hold, or have held; the Dates of Appointments; and published writings for which they are distinguished, etc., together with the various Acts of Parliament relating to the Medical Profession at large, price 6s.

The Medical Register and Directory of the United States of America. Containing the Names and Addresses of about 70,000 Practitioners. Second issue, price 30s.

Anuario del Comercio. Commercial Directory for Spain, its Colonies and Dependencies. Containing 500,000 Names and Addresses of the Commercial Houses, Public Officers, Offices, etc., etc. Annual, price 20s. net.

32

** Single copies of any work sent post free in the United Kingdom on receipt of published price.

Any work not on this Catalogue, will be procured and sent immediately on receipt of order with remittance or reference.

Special terms made for large purchases, the furnishing of libraries, and shipping orders.

Messrs. Baillière, Tindall, and Cox have special facilities for the disposal of author's works in the United States, and abroad; being in almost daily communication with the principal houses and agents.

Messrs. Baillière, Tindall, and Cox are the specially appointed Agents for "The Revue des Deux Mondes."

Revue Scientifique de la France et de l'Etranger.
Revue Politique et Litteraire.
Revue Philosophique de la France et de l'Etranger.
Revue Mensuelle de Medecine et de Chirurgie.
Le Progres Medical.

The Following Valuable Scientific Dictionaries are in course of Publication in French.

	£	s.	d.
Dictionnaire de Chimie pure et appliquée, en livraisons	0	4	6
Dictionnaire de Medecine, de chirurgie, et d'hygiène vétérinaires. Edition entièrement	3	0	0

refondue par A. Zundel, en 6 parties

Dictionnaire Encyclopedique des Sciences Médicales publié par demi-volume de chacun 400 pages et en quatre séries simultanées: la premiere, commençant par la lettre A; la deuxième, par la lettre L; la troisième, par la lettre Q, et la quatrième par F.   0 6 0

Nouveau Dictionnaire de Medecine et de chirurgie pratiques, d'environ 32 volumes, chaque   0 10 0

CPSIA information can be obtained
at www.ICGtesting.com
Printed in the USA
FSHW021351030919
61672FS